Men-at-Arms • 106

Napoleon's German Allies (4)

Bavaria

Otto von Pivka • Illustrated by Richard Hook

First published in Great Britain in 1980 by Osprey Publishing,
PO Box 883, Oxford, OX1 9PL, UK
PO Box 3985, New York, NY 10185-3985, USA
Email: info@ospreypublishing.com

Osprey Publishing, part of Bloomsbury Publishing Plc

Transferred to digital print on demand 2016.

First published 1980.
12th impression 2002.

Printed and bound in Great Britain

A CIP catalogue record for this book is available from the British Library.

ISBN: 978 0 85045 373 7

Filmset in Great Britain.

Acknowledgements
I would like to express my sincere thanks to all those people and institutions which gave such generous assistance to me in the preparation of this book. They include the Directors and Staffs of the Staatliche Museum für Preussische Kulturbesitz (Lipperheide Sammlung) in Berlin; the Bavarian Army Museum in Ingolstadt (particulaarly Frau Rotraud Wrede); the Zentralbibliothek der Bundeswehr in Düsseldorf and the Bavarian Staatsarchiv-Kriegsarchiv in München. (Otto von Pivka, Nürnberg, August 1979)

Bibliography
Bezzel, Oskar, *Die Geschichte des Bayerischen Heeres*
Knötel and Sieg, *Handbuch der Uniformkunde*, Hamburg 1937
Knötel, R., *Lose Blätter zur Uniformkunde*
Knötel, R., *Mitheilungen zur Lose Blätter*
Müller and Braun, *Organisations—und Uniformierungsgeschichte des Bayerischen Heeres 1806–1906*
Documents and exhibits in museums and archives in Berlin, München and Ingolstadt.

Introduction

In 1792 Bavaria consisted of the following territories: Electorate of Bavaria, Electorate of the Rhineland Palatinate, Upper Palatinate, Zweibrücken, and the duchies of Berg and Jülich (around Köln and Aachen).

Within the boundaries of Bavaria itself were certain independent cities of the Holy Roman Empire such as Nürnberg and Augsburg, as well as various ecclesiastical estates such as the bishoprics of Passau, Freising and Eichstadt. Bavaria was thus fragmented among the hundreds of other tiny German states of the period, and was too weak and diffuse to carry much weight in political, economic or military terms. Traditionally she had allied herself with France, as in Marlborough's time, the War of the Austrian Succession (1740–48), the Seven Years War (1756–63) and in the War of the Bavarian Succession (1778–79). In January 1742 the Elector of Bavaria, Carl Albrecht, had managed to secure for himself the title of Holy Roman Emperor, but his reign was brief and ineffective.

Member states of the Holy Roman Empire were required to furnish armed contingents to fight for the Imperial cause in time of war, and it was in this way that Bavarian troops were mobilized in 1792: this time to oppose the armies of Revolutionary France. By October of that year, however, Bavaria had declared her neutrality in the struggle. By 1796 the cohesion of the Holy Roman Empire had suffered so much that the fighting ceased to permit diplomats from all the warring states to meet at the Congress of Rastatt (in Baden) to redraw the map of Germany. This revision was strongly in favour of France, who had taken the Spanish Netherlands (Belgium), Alsace, Lorraine and many other areas on the left bank of the Rhine by force of arms. The Congress was to compensate dispossessed rulers of territories so lost with other lands from within the remains of the Empire.

War broke out again, however, when the French representatives at the Congress were murdered by Austrian agents while on a journey, and fighting continued until December 1800, when the French decisively defeated the polyglot Imperial forces at the battle of Hohenlinden, east of München. On 24 March 1803 the ruling body of the Empire (*Reichsdeputation*) met to carry out a major reform of the Imperial administrative

Maximilian Joseph, King of Bavaria 1805–15; Kurfürst, 1799–1805. It was this man's fortune to rule in a period when Bavaria rose from a weak, fragmented electorate of the Holy Roman Empire to a kingdom which stretched from Franconia in central Germany to present-day Italy. Bavaria threw in her lot with France during the Revolutionary Wars, and abandoned Napoleon early enough in 1813 to preserve most of her gains against a vengeful Austria.

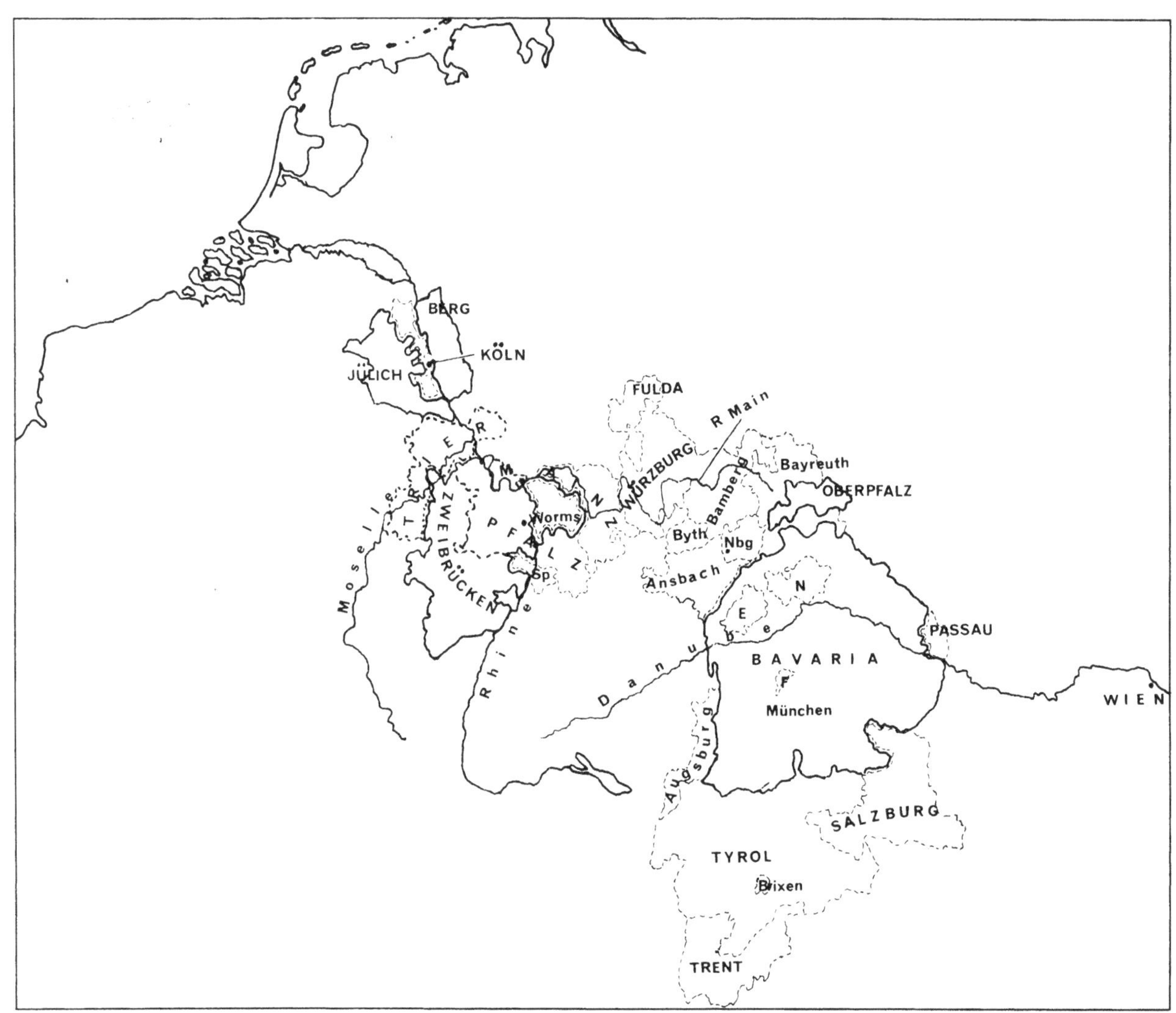

The electorate of Bavaria, 1792; the fragmented nature of the state was by no means unusual in the Germany of that time. Some principalities were so small that their military contingents amounted only to a company of men. The later additions to Bavaria are shown in dotted lines. Abbreviations: Byth = part of principality of Bayreuth; E = bishopric of Eichstadt; F = bishopric of Freising; M = bishopric of Mainz; N = principality of Neuburg; Nbg = Imperial city of Nürnberg; Sp = bishopric of Speier.

structure. All free Imperial cities lost their status and were incorporated into neighbouring states, with the exception of Hamburg, Bremen, Lübeck, Frankfurt am Main, Nürnberg and Augsburg. The dozens of tiny ecclesiastical states were treated in the same manner. Bavaria profited by gaining the bishoprics of Passau, Freising, Augsburg, Bamberg and Würzburg, all of which brought with them their own tiny military contingents. As a result of this reshuffle the Electors of Köln and Trier vanished and were replaced by those of Salzburg, Württemberg, Baden and Hessen-Kassel. (The Electors chose the head of the Holy Roman Empire—traditionally an Austrian, and at that date Franz II. The other Electors were those of Brandenburg, Bohemia, Saxony, Hannover and the archbishop of Mainz.)

Napoleon, who had now dignified his military dictatorship over France by assuming the title of Emperor, saw that the greatest safety for his country lay in transforming the jumble of small German states east of the Rhine into a *cordon sanitaire* against his most immediately threatening continental enemies, Austria and Prussia. Austria presented him with the ideal opportunity when she attacked Bavaria in 1805. Napoleon destroyed both the Austrian and Prussian armies in a brilliant campaign culminating in the envelopment of the incompetent Austrian General Mack and his subsequent capitulation at Ulm on 20 October 1805, and the immensely destructive battle of Austerlitz on 2 December. Bavaria, Baden and Württemberg had allied themselves with France in this campaign, and they were now richly rewarded for their services.

Bavaria gained the status of kingdom and the territories of Tyrol, Voralberg, Brixen and Trent from Austria, but lost Würzburg to the Archduke Ferdinand (who relinquished Salzburg to Austria). The Elector of Württemberg also became a king, and the Elector of Baden became a grand duke. In 1806 the free cities of Augsburg and Nürnberg also fell to Bavaria; but she lost Jülich and Berg to provide Joachim Murat with a grand duchy in northern Germany. Eugene de Beauharnais, viceroy of Italy, married Augusta, the daughter of the king of Bavaria. Various other matrimonial plots further secured Napoleon's hold on his new vassal states. On 12 July 1806 he decreed the formation of the Confederation of the Rhine, which eventually included all German states except Prussia, as well as France and (in 1807) the Grand Duchy of Warsaw. In August 1806 the rulers of German states in the Confederation left the Holy Roman Empire, and the Emperor Franz II became 'Franz I of Austria'.

In 1806 Napoleon crushed Prussia at the twin battles of Jena and Auerstädt; abolished Hessen-Kassel, Brunswick and Hannover; and created the Kingdom of Westfalia out of these and other lands.

In the 1809 campaign against Austria, Bavaria was again a front-line state, and many of the preliminary actions took place on her soil. The campaign saw Napoleon's defeat at Aspern-Essling. His subsequent victories at Wagram and the battle of Znaim retrieved the situation, however, and Austria was again humbled. The Tyrol rose in revolt against Bavaria, and it was months before it could be pacified. As a result of the diplomatic negotiations in the aftermath of this war Bavaria gained Salzburg but lost Trent.

In 1812 Bavaria provided a corps (the VI) for the Russian campaign; but in 1813 she abandoned Napoleon's cause before the battle of Liepzig, and fought his retreating army at the battle of Hanau in an unsuccessful attempt to cut it off from France. In 1814 the Tyrol was handed back to Austria, as was Salzburg in 1815, but Bavaria gained Würzburg and much of Frankfurt am Main as a result of the Congress of Vienna.

Uniforms and Organization 1792-99

In 1785 the Bavarian War Minister émigré American loyalist, Benjamin Thompson—later ennobled by Maximilian Joseph of Bavaria as the Graf von Rumford) had introduced a revolutionary uniform system into the Bavarian army. Its hallmarks were distinctive style and great economy, and it was worn until 1799.

Queen Caroline, wife of Maximilian Joseph. Like many other reigning families, the Wittelsbachs of Bavaria allied themselves by marriage to the Bonapartes; Auguste, daughter of Maximilian Joseph and Caroline, married Prince Eugene, Viceroy of Italy.

The old felt bicorn continued to be worn by officers off duty and at court, but for other purposes army headdress was a black leather, low-crowned helmet with a hair crest falling to the rear. The brass front plate extended across the front of the helmet and rose to a peak in the form of a lion's head. Below this were the arms of Bavaria under an electoral cap, and at each side was a large brass disc holding the black leather chinstrap. The large front peak was horizontal and extended around the sides and rear of the helmet in narrower form. The hair crest was white for officers of the general staff, commandants, and for grenadiers and cavalry; it was black for Feldjägers, Füsiliers, fortress troops and invalides. Hair was powdered, rolled and queued and bound in a pigtail. Cavalry troopers wore moustaches.

The new coat was in two patterns: a long-skirted type for officers, and a very short-skirted version for soldiers. The collar was two inches high and closed to the top; half-lapels were worn folded back, and the lower portion of the coat front was cut away to show a false waistcoat. The cuffs were round and plain for all except the cavalry, who had them with a 'V'-shaped cut-out along the top.

The Rumford Kasket, worn by all arms and ranks of the Bavarian army from 1790 to 1799. Of 'American parentage', it was light and practical, shielding the eyes and neck from the weather; but it was unpopular with the Bavarian military establishment because it was not sufficiently flamboyant, and the hair crest, when wet, made the wearers 'look like savages'. (Bavarian Army Museum, Ingolstadt)

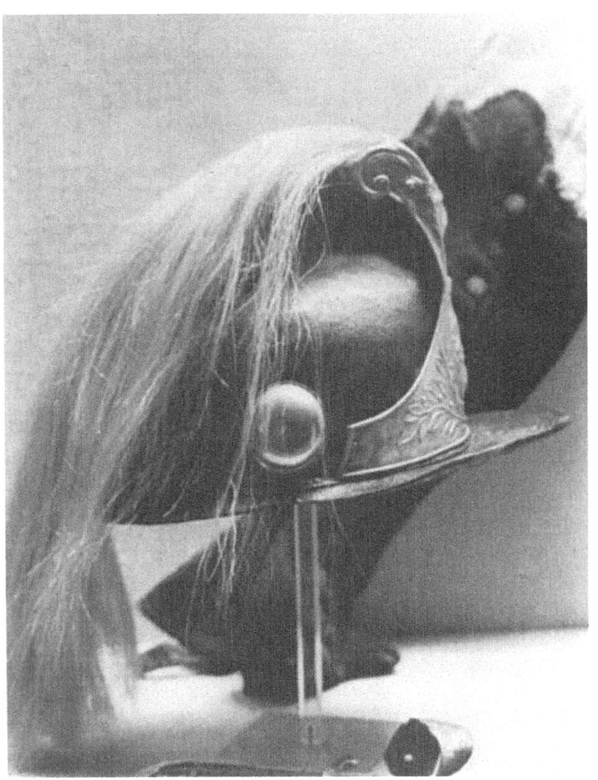

Facing colours were worn on the collar, half-lapels, cuffs and turnbacks by infantry. Dragoons, Kürassiers and Chevau-Légers had collars in the coat colour, and turnbacks in the coat colour edged with cloth in the facing colour about one and a half inches wide. The half-lapels were held with five buttons for soldiers, the number of buttons varying with rank for officers. On the shoulders were black leather *contre-epaulettes* with brass crescents at the outer ends and with brass chains around the strap. No stock was worn, but a white linen band was attached to the shirt collar, and this projected above the coat collar and gave the impression of a conventional stock. Reflecting the economic principles of this uniform, the soldiers' grey trousers were sewn to the black gaiters, which had Hungarian-pattern tops with a black tassel and which closed with black leather buttons. Officers wore grey breeches, black boots and short yellow gloves.

The coat-tails bore horizontal, three-button pocket flaps and there were two buttons at the rear of the waist. The cuffs had two buttons at the rear seam. Coat colour varied according to regiment as follows: generals, general staff, commandants, infantry of the line, Kürassiers and dragoons—white; Hartschiere (royal bodyguard), Trabanten (palace guards), artillery, engineers, train, garrison troops and military academy—dark blue; Feldjäger (rifles) and Chevau-Légers—green.

The officers' badges of rank were worn according to the following system. The top lapel button and the bottom two were always worn, and the other two buttons were added according to rank. Generals wore five lapel buttons each with the buttonhole embroidered in gold or silver (the button colour) with tassels at the outer ends. Those generals who were also colonels-in-chief (Chef or Inhaber) of a regiment had in addition one buttonhole to either side of the collar.

Lieutenant-generals had four lapel buttons with embroidered buttonholes and tassels; major-generals had three. This scheme was repeated for field officers (colonel, lieutenant-colonel and major), but there were no tassels and the buttonholes were edged in plain gold/silver lace. Junior officers (captain, first lieutenant, second lieutenant) used the same scheme again, but their lapel buttonholes were edged in silk in the button colour. All officers wore silver and light blue sword knots with a silver tassel. They carried malacca canes with a gold knob and silver cords.

The rank badge system for soldiers was also shown on the lapels but they all wore five buttons, the differences being in the number of buttonholes embroidered in the button colour, as follows: sergeant-major—five (he also carried a gold-topped cane and wore a white and light blue sabre knot with a red wreath). Staff sergeant—top four buttonholes embroidered; cane and white and light blue sabre-strap. Sergeant—top three buttonholes; cane and white and light blue sabre-strap. Corporal—top two buttonholes, hazelwood stick, white and light blue sabre strap. Lance-corporal—top buttonhole only.

In addition the regimental saddler and the drum-major had their top buttonholes embroidered with a white Hungarian knot in camel hair, and the drum-major's facings were edged in white and light blue diced braid. From October 1791 the drum-major wore a bandolier in the facing colour edged in gold or silver according to the button colour, and bearing a gold/silver plate with the crowned monogram of the colonel-in-chief. The swallow's nests (in the facing colour) also bore this crest. The provost had only three lapel buttons, the top one having a white or yellow Hungarian knot buttonhole. The adjutant, quartermaster, chief clerk, surgeon, under-surgeon and ensign or cornet all had the top buttonhole embroidered in plaited gold or silver thread; the chief clerk, surgeon and under-surgeon had seven lapel buttons, the quartermaster eight. Surgeons wore dark blue coats and lapels with scarlet linings, collar and cuffs, scarlet waistcoat and black trousers. Cavalry blacksmiths wore normal facings, five lapel buttons, but iron grey coats and trousers.

Drummers and trumpeters wore light blue and

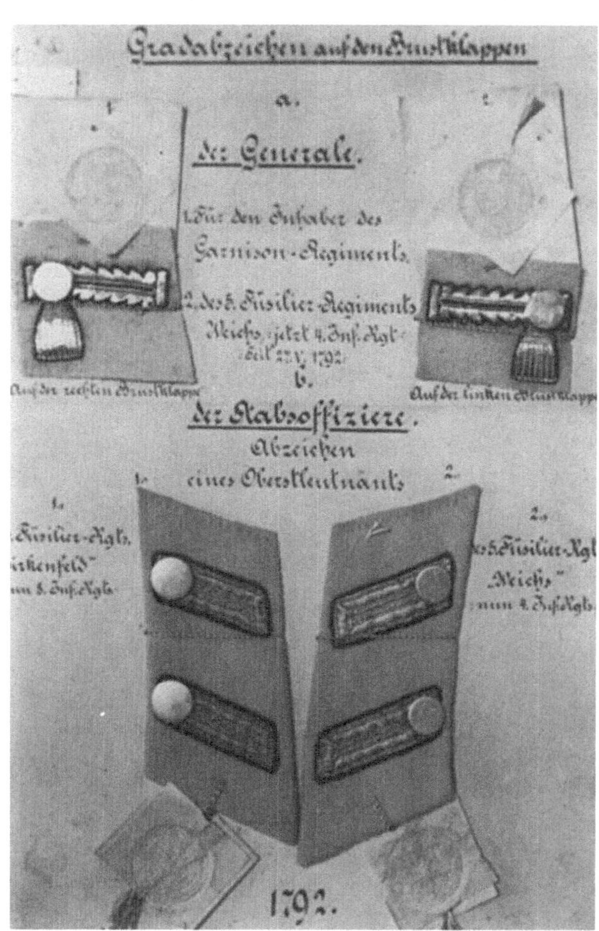

Sealed patterns for lapel lace, 1790–99. These rare displays show the approved buttonhole embroidery for generals (top) and field officers, worn on the lapels of Rumford's new-style uniforms. (Bavarian Army Museum)

white diced lace edging to collar, lapels, cuffs, turnbacks, lapel buttonholes and to the swallow's nests, which were in the facing colour. Musicians' lace was light blue and silver. The flat buttons also bore badges according to rôle as follows: grenadiers—the regimental number flanked by two grenades; Füsiliers—the regimental number; Jägers—a hunting horn; cavalry—the regimental number; artillery—a cannon (in 1799 this was changed to crossed gun barrels over a pyramid of cannon balls); engineers—plan view of a fortress with small flanking redoubts; garrison troops—a tower.

In barracks and off duty infantry officers could wear a long-skirted, single-breasted grey frock coat with collar and cuffs in the regimental facing colour. Feldjäger officers could wear similar

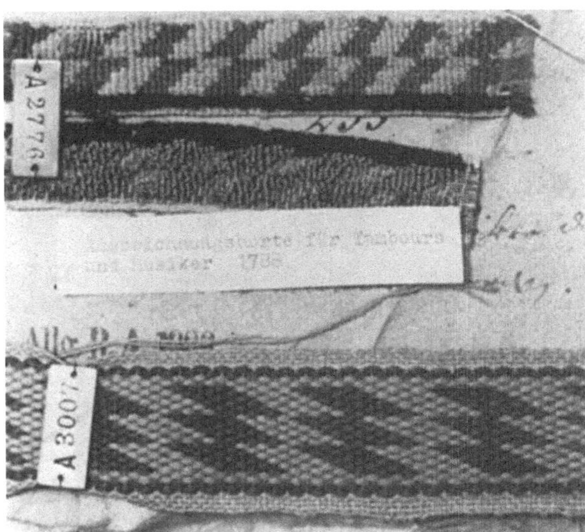

Sealed patterns for drummers' and musicians' lace, 1788–99. The light blue and white lozenge pattern has been connected with Bavaria for centuries, and is still to be seen in state heraldry at every level. (Top) Drummers (centre) Musicians, light blue and silver (bottom) Unidentified. (Bavarian Army Museum)

coats, but the collar, cuffs and front edges were piped green; and their duty uniform coats were short-skirted in the same style as worn by the soldiers. Their facings were of black velvet.

Greatcoats were ash grey for the infantry, with a standing collar; they were mid-calf length, with epaulettes and rank badges as on the tunic. Feldjäger officers had green overcoats with black collars.

All cavalrymen wore short yellow gloves, and Kürassiers and dragoons wore buff leather breeches and high, cuffed boots; Chevau-Légers wore grey breeches. Saddle furniture for Kürassiers and dragoons was red with light blue and white diced edging; for Chevau-Légers it was grey with white edging. Harness was black.

Equipment consisted of white leather belts (black for Feldjäger), plain black pouches, a sabre and musket. Dragoons carried infantry muskets and heavy, straight-bladed swords (Pallasch); Kürassiers wore no cuirasses and carried the Pallasch and a brace of pistols. The brown calfskin pack of the infantry was carried on a single strap on the left hip, slung over the right shoulder. The strapping was white for all except Feldjäger, who had black. When on campaign as part of the Imperial Austrian forces, all ranks wore a white armband on the upper left arm (1792–1800).

Organization in 1790

The infantry was organized into four grenadier and 14 Füsilier regiments, the former being formed by concentrating the two grenadier companies in each old infantry regiment together. Regiments which retained grenadier companies had to retitle them as follows: 1st Grenadier Company—'Leib-Compagnie'; 2nd Grenadier Company—'Obersts Compagnie'. In addition there were two Feldjäger regiments. Each regiment had two battalions of four companies and in peace-time each company was 150 men strong: three officers, eight NCOs, three drummers, one company quartermaster sergeant, one pioneer, eight lance-corporals and 126 privates. When mobilized this increased by one second lieutenant, one pioneer, four lance-corporals and 12 privates. Two battalions formed a 'brigade' for tactical purposes. The cavalry consisted of a Kürassier brigade of two regiments, two Chevau-Légers brigades (one of two regiments and one of one) and three regiments of dragoons. Each regiment had four squadrons of 150 men in peace-time, 180 men when mobilized (but only had horses sufficient to mount one squadron).

The artillery had two battalions each of four companies with the following peace establishment: one captain (battery commander), two lieutenants, one staff sergeant, one quartermaster sergeant, four sergeants, eight corporals, two drummers, 16 lance-corporals and 115 gunners. They served six cannon and two howitzers.

In 1792 Thompson was created Graf von Rumford and appointed colonel-in-chief of the artillery; he designed and produced the Rumford 3pdr. cannon which came into service in 1794. In 1795 Austrian-pattern 6pdr. cannon and 7pdr. howitzers were introduced, and in 1797 12pdr. siege guns were also issued. The guns were bronze and were mounted on grey carriages with black metal parts. In common with other states at this time there was no permanent artillery train and at time of mobilization horses were detached from the cavalry to move the guns, with civilian drivers. Battery techniques were unknown, and

Table of Facings 1790–99

Leibgarde der Trabanten (Palace Guards)—silver-edged bicorn; dark blue coat, black collar, cuffs and lapels all edged silver, the coat lined white and trimmed silver; white waistcoat, breeches and gaiters; black shoes, white gloves, silver buttons.

Regiment	*Facings*	*Buttons*
1st Grenadier und Leib-Infanterie-Regt.	light blue	white
2nd Grenadier-Regt. 'Kurprinz'	light blue	yellow
3rd Grenadier-Regt. 'Graf Ysenburg'	dark blue	white
4th Grenadier-Regt. 'Baden'	dark blue	yellow
1st Füsilier-Regt. 'Herzog von Zweibrücken'	red	white
2nd Füsilier-Regt. 'Prinz Wilhelm von Birkenfeld'	red	yellow
3rd Füsilier-Regt. 'Rodenhausen'	brick red	white
4th Füsilier-Regt. 'de la Motte'	brick red	yellow
5th Füsilier-Regt. 'von Wahl'	yellow	white
6th Füsilier-Regt. 'Pfalzgraf Max'	yellow	yellow
7th Füsilier-Regt. 'von Zedtwitz'	green	white
8th Füsilier-Regt. 'von Rambaldi'	green	yellow
9th Füsilier-Regt. 'von Weichs'	peach red	white
10th Füsilier-Regt. 'Joseph Hohenhausen'	peach red	yellow
11th Füsilier-Regt. 'von Preysing'	crimson	white
12th Füsilier-Regt. 'von Belderbusch'	crimson	yellow
13th Füsilier-Regt. 'Moritz von Isenburg'	black	white
14th Füsilier-Regt. 'von Kling'	black	yellow
1st Feldjäger-Regt. 'von Schweicheldt'	black	white
2nd Feldjäger-Regt. 'Fürst Ysenburg'	black	yellow

Leibgarde der Hartschiere (Royal Bodyguard)—silver-edged bicorn with high light blue-over-white plume; dark blue coat, no collar, black lapels and cuffs edged silver, silver coat edging and buttons; yellow waistcoat, buff breeches, high, cuffed boots with white knee cuffs.

Cavalry Facings 1790–99	*Facings*	*Buttons*
1st Kürassier-Regt. 'Minucci'	scarlet	white
2nd Kürassier-Regt. 'Winckelhausen'	scarlet	yellow
1st Dragoner-Regt. 'Leib-Dragoner'	black	white
2nd Dragoner-Regt. 'Fürst Taxis'	black	yellow
1st Chevau-Légers-Regt. 'Prinz Leiningen'	black	white
2nd Chevau-Légers-Regt. 'La Rosée'	black	yellow
3rd Chevau-Légers-Regt. 'Wahl'	apple green	white
Artillery	black	yellow
Engineers	black	yellow

the guns were distributed in groups of two to each infantry battalion.

Battle History 1792–1800

1792 Patrol duty along Franco-Bavarian borders.

1793 War against France as part of the forces of the Holy Roman Empire.

Order of Battle (as part of the Army of the Upper Rhine)

1st Füsiliers, 6th Füsiliers, 1st and 2nd Feldjägers — each with two artillery pieces

One combined cavalry regiment (3 squadrons) made up as follows:

1st Chevau-Légers—2 squadrons
2nd Chevau-Légers—1 squadron
3rd Chevau-Légers—50 troopers

One combined battalion, 4th Füsiliers and 60 mounted troopers of the 2nd Kürassiers were attached to the Army of the Lower Rhine which saw no action this year and very little in 1794–96.

Battle participation, Army of the Upper Rhine contingent:

May 1793—siege of Mainz; July—combats to ward off the French armies of the

Rhine and the Maas; October—storming of the Weissenburg Lines (west of the Rhine, north of Strassburg). The Prussian and Imperial troops cleared the Lines and then occupied them as winter quarters, building a further blocking position to the west. On 18 December the French attacked this new line; fighting went on until 22 December, when they broke through the Bavarian position at Fröschweiler. The Prussian and Imperial troops fell back north to Mannheim and abandoned the siege of Landau fortress. Bavaria thus lost the Rhineland Palatinate.

1794 Upper Rhine: 24 May—crossed the Rhine at Mannheim following Prussian success in battle of Kaiserslautern (23 May). 22 July—sent to Worms. 13 August—Bavarians reinforced with a combined battalion, 5th Füsiliers, three 6pdr. cannon, a 7pdr. howitzer and two companies, 1st Feldjägers.

The Chevau-Légers and the complete Feldjäger battalion were now attached to Major-General von Blücher's Prussian brigade from August to October. They fought in the successful clashes of Friedelsheim (28 August), Battenberg (5 September), Herzheim (13 September), Monsheim (16 October), and Zell (17 October).

On 19 October Prussia concluded a separate peace with France and withdrew her army from the Rhine; the Imperial forces were thus left with no alternative but to fall back east of that river as well. The Bavarians were reinforced on 12 October by two companies of Feldjägers. On 20 October the Bavarians entered Mainz to become part of its garrison, but the Chevau-Légers were soon sent out into the country east of that city.

1795 Nothing of consequence for the Bavarian contingent.

1796 Nothing of consequence for the Bavarian contingent.

1797–1800 Bavaria maintained neutrality.

The 1799 Reorganization

The Bavarian army was reorganized in 1799 and the infantry regiments were regrouped as follows:

Old Title	*New Title 1799* (with the numbering as introduced in 1806)
1st Grenadiers	1st Linien-Infanterie-Leib-Regt.
2nd Grenadiers	2nd Linien-Infanterie-Regt. 'Kurprinz'
3rd Grenadiers	Disbanded 1799
4th Grenadiers	Disbanded 1799
1st Füsiliers	6th Linien-Infanterie-Regt. 'Herzog Wilhelm'
2nd Füsiliers	3rd Linien-Infanterie-Regt. 'Herzog Karl'
3rd Füsiliers	9th Linien-Infanterie-Regt. 'Graf von Ysenburg'
4th Füsiliers	11th Linien-Infanterie-Regt. 'Schlossberg'
5th Füsiliers	4th Linien-Infanterie-Regt. 'vacant von Weichs'
6th Füsiliers	8th Linien-Infanterie-Regt. 'Herzog Pius'
7th Füsiliers	Disbanded 1799
8th Füsiliers	7th Linien-Infanterie-Regt. 'Zedtwitz-Stengel'
9th Füsiliers	5th Linien-Infanterie-Regt. 'Graugeben'
10th Füsiliers	Disbanded 1799
11th Füsiliers	10th Linien-Infanterie-Regt. 'von Junker'
12th Füsiliers	Disbanded 1799
13th Füsiliers	Disbanded 1799
14th Füsiliers	Disbanded 1799
1st Feldjägers	Light Battalions Metzen No. 1 and Clossmann No. 2
2nd Feldjägers	Light Battalions 1st Salern No. 3 and 2nd Salern No. 4

Uniforms and Organization 1799-1815

Graf von Rumford's novel uniforms, although copied by Württemberg and by the émigré French army of the Prince of Condé, proved to be too foreign to survive in Bavaria and in 1799 they were replaced by a more traditional style of clothing.

For the infantry this consisted of a very high

leather helmet (the Raupenhelm) with black caterpillar crest, lambskin for privates and corporals, bearskin for senior NCOs and officers. The oval brass front plate bore the cypher 'MJ' ('MJK' from 1806) and was surmounted by the electoral cap (a royal crown from 1806). Over the peak was a wide brass band with a star in the centre, terminating in round brass chinstrap bosses holding the black leather chinstrap, which was edged in fine brass chains. To either side of the oval brass plates was a small brass stud (a lion's mask for officers from 1805), and a fine brass chain led from the chinstrap bosses up to the studs and hung below the front plate. The front and rear peaks were plain leather for soldiers, but those of officers were edged in gold. Until 1805 officers wore the old-fashioned bicorn with wide edging in the button colour, brooch, loop, button and light blue and silver hat tassels.

Company Distinctions

Grenadiers wore a red cut-feather plume over the left chinstrap boss. In 1811 the Schützen-Kompanie (light or sharpshooter company) adopted a similar plume in green. For the 2nd Bns. of each regiment the lower half of these plumes were white; from 1814 the élite companies of the new 3rd Bns. had black lower halves to the plumes. The Füsilier companies wore small worsted tufts above the left boss as follows: Leib-Kompanie (from 1811 '1st Füsilier-Kompanie')—white; Oberst-Kompanie (2nd Füsilier)—white and yellow: Oberstleutnant (3rd Füsilier)—green; 1st Majors-Kompanie (4th Füsilier)—green and yellow; 2nd Majors-Kompanie (5th Füsiliers)—red. At the end of July 1814 the company tufts for Füsiliers of the 1st Bn. of each regiment were changed to plain colours (white, yellow, green, blue, red respectively); those of 2nd Bns. had white lower halves, and those of 3rd Bns. had black lower halves.

Rank Badges 1799–1802

From 1799 to 1802 infantry officers wore no readily identifiable schematic badges of rank. Generals wore very wide silver and light blue waist sashes with silver bullion tassels, and portepées (sabre straps) of the same materials. Field officers had very wide silver and light blue silk waist sashes with thin silver fringes, and their portepée tassels were also thin. Junior officers had thinner waist sashes. Rank was also indicated by the amount of ivory decoration on the canes. NCOs showed their ranks by their sticks and by their blue and white sabre straps as before.

The coat was now in the traditional Bavarian cornflower blue colour, with full lapels, standing collar, shoulder-straps and short skirts for soldiers, long skirts and no shoulder-straps for officers. Facings were worn on collar, lapels, cuffs and piping as shown in the following table. Turnbacks were red, shoulder-straps were in the coat colour piped red. Waistcoats and breeches were white, gaiters black. Bandoliers were white and the pack was worn as before (on the back with two straps over the shoulders from 1808).

Collar and cuff details, 1790–99, traced from official pattern books. The collar bears the special lace embroidery worn by colonels-in-chief of regiments. The infantry cuff was of plain round (Swedish) style, while the cavalry had a V-shaped cut-out at the top. Buttons are 1.5cm in diameter; the cuffs are 8.2cm deep (infantry) and 4cm (cavalry, centre of cut-out). (Bavarian War Archives)

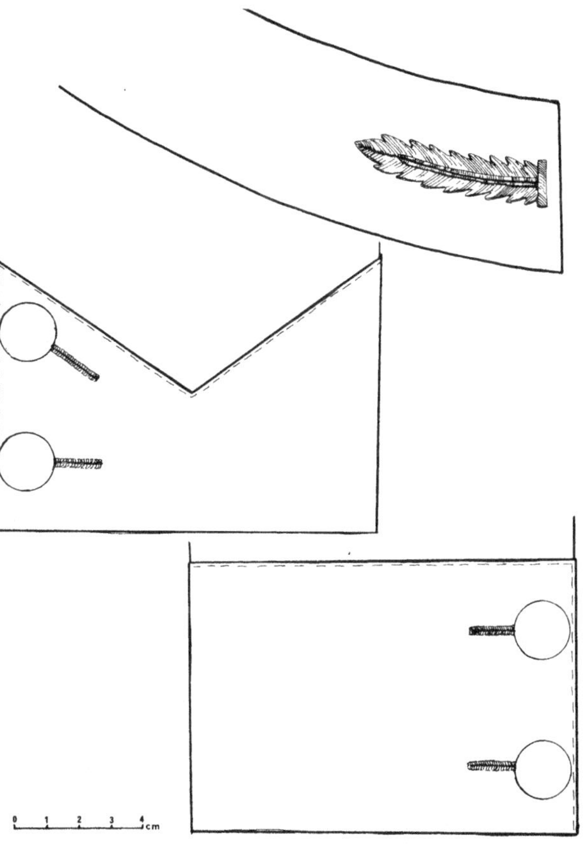

Detail sketch of the plate on a surviving Rumford helmet in the Bavarian Army Museum, Ingolstadt.

The system of rank badges was changed in 1799 for cavalry and artillery, and from 1802 was adopted also by the infantry. Generals wore white, cut-feather edging to their bicorns and elaborate gold embroidery to collar, cuffs and coat fronts. Field officers wore regimental uniform with a gold or silver edging to the top and front of the collar and three broad gold or silver stripes on each side for colonel, two for lieutenant-colonel and one for major. Junior officers had no edging to the collar but the three, two and one stripes for captain down to second lieutenant. From 1804 officers wore white gloves. Until 1810 mounted infantry officers had saddle furniture in the facing colour, thereafter red with silver edging. The waist sashes were light blue and silver, as were the sword straps; the canes were retained.

The NCOs had the same system of collar rank badges, but in the button colour instead of gold, and they carried the same canes and sabre straps as from 1790–99. Until 1804 NCOs carried spontoons, thereafter firearms.

Infantry Uniforms 1799–1815

The regimental facings in 1799 were as follows (numbers were not used from 1799 to 1806; the 1806 numbers can be seen in brackets after the names).

Regiment (and subsequent changes of title)	*Facings*	*Buttons*
'Leib-Regiment' (1) (1811 'König')	Black (red from 1802) with white buttonhole laces, 7 on each lapel, 4 on each cuff, 2 at the rear waist.	white
'Kurprinz' (2) (1806 'Kronprinz')	Black (red from 1802) with wide yellow buttonhole laces as above.	yellow
'Herzog Karl' (3) (1806 'Prinz Karl')	red	yellow
'vacant von Weichs' (4) (1804 'Salern'; 1811 'Sachsen-Hildburghausen')	sulphur yellow	white
'Graugeben' (5) (1800 'von Preysing')	pink with red edging	white
'Herzog Wilhelm' (6)	red	white
'Zedtwitz-Stengel' (7) (1804 'von Morawitsky'; 1806 'Löwenstein-Wertheim')	white	yellow
'Herzog Pius' (8)	sulphur yellow	yellow
'Graf von Ysenburg' (9)	scarlet	yellow
'von Junker' (10) (1800 'Pompei-Dalwigk'; 1804 'Junker')	crimson	white
'Schlossberg' (11) (1801 'von Kinkel') (This regiment was transferred to the Grand Duchy of Berg in 1806.)	orange	yellow
'von Löwenstein-Wertheim' (12) (Raised 1803, disbanded 1806)	orange	white

By 1806 the regimental facings had changed as follows: 1st and 2nd Regiments—red; 3rd—white piping added to collar; 4th—red piping added to facings; 5th—no change; 6th—white piping added to facings; 7th—facings changed to pink (in 1803); 8th—red piping added to facings; 9th and 10th—collars changed to poppy red, lapels and cuffs yellow with red piping; the new 11th (1807–11)—collar poppy red, lapels and cuffs green with red piping, buttons white; 12th (disbanded 1806)—no change; 13th (raised 1805)—red collar, black facings piped red, white buttons; 14th (raised 1806)—red collar, black facings piped red, yellow buttons.

The 11th Regiment was transferred in 1806 to the newly formed Grand Duchy of Berg (see my Men-at-Arms book *Napoleon's German Allies (1)*); a new 11th Regiment was raised in 1807 and disbanded in 1811. In 1811 the 13th Regiment was renumbered 11th and the 14th became the 13th.

On 15 April 1812 infantry officers discarded the sash and received instead the silver gorget with gold crest as a badge of office.

In 1814 all infantry regiments' facings became red and their buttons yellow with the regimental number on them. In this year new 12th and 14th Regiments were raised, as were the Garde-Grenadier. The 1st and 2nd Regiments lost their distinctive buttonhole lace decoration at this point. Light company (Schützen) turnbacks were decorated with green hunting horns enclosing the yellow regimental number.

From 1805 field and junior officers also wore the Raupenhelm.

Drummers had large red plumes on the left side of the helmet, just above the light blue and white cockade. Their facings and sleeve seams were edged in wide lace in the button colour, as were the swallow's nests at the top of each sleeve,

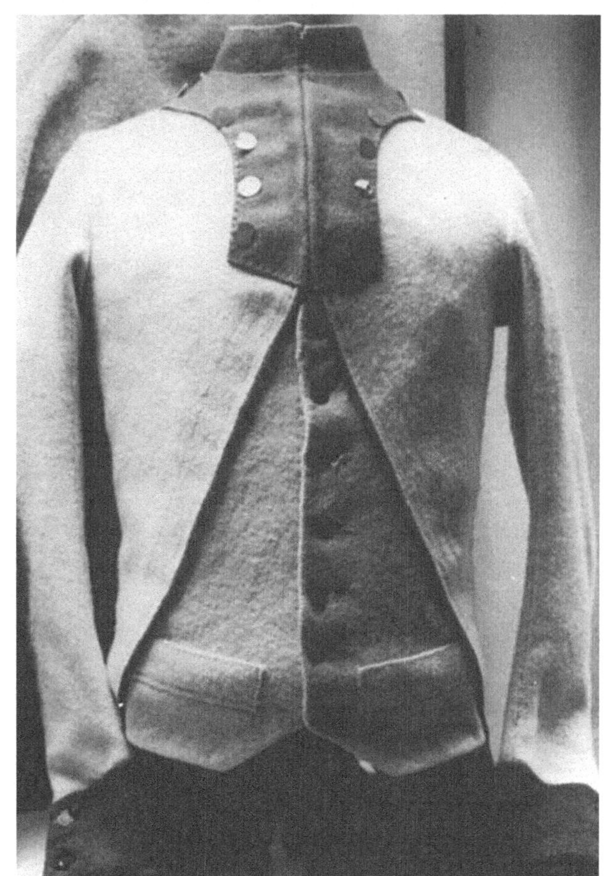

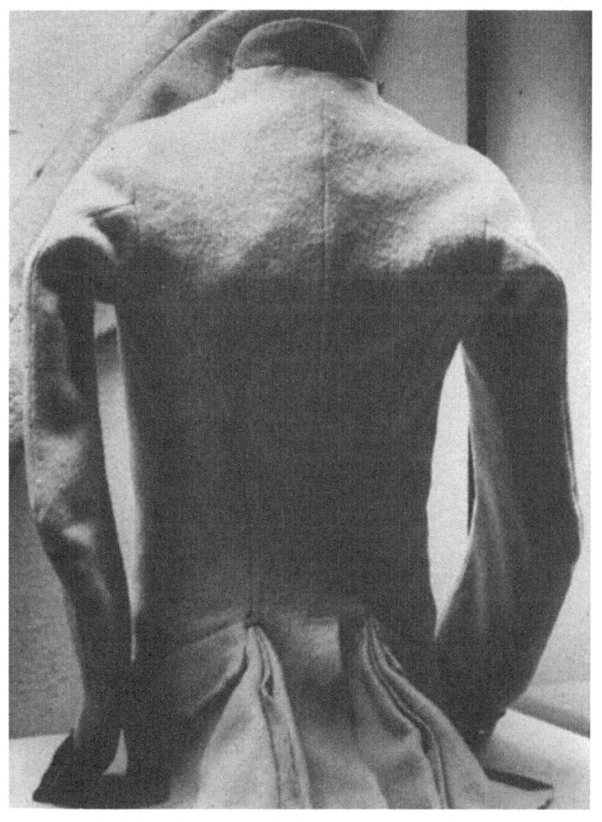

Rumford infantry coat, 1790–99; front and rear views. Note false waistcoat; relatively tiny lapels; plain white metal buttons; skirts turned back to expose blue lining at the front only; false waistcoat pockets; and position of epaulette buttons, visible on the base of the collar in the rear view—the epaulettes themselves are missing. The length of the exposed section of false waistcoat is noticeable—it is often shown too small in paintings executed at later dates, even by Knötel. (Bavarian Army Museum)

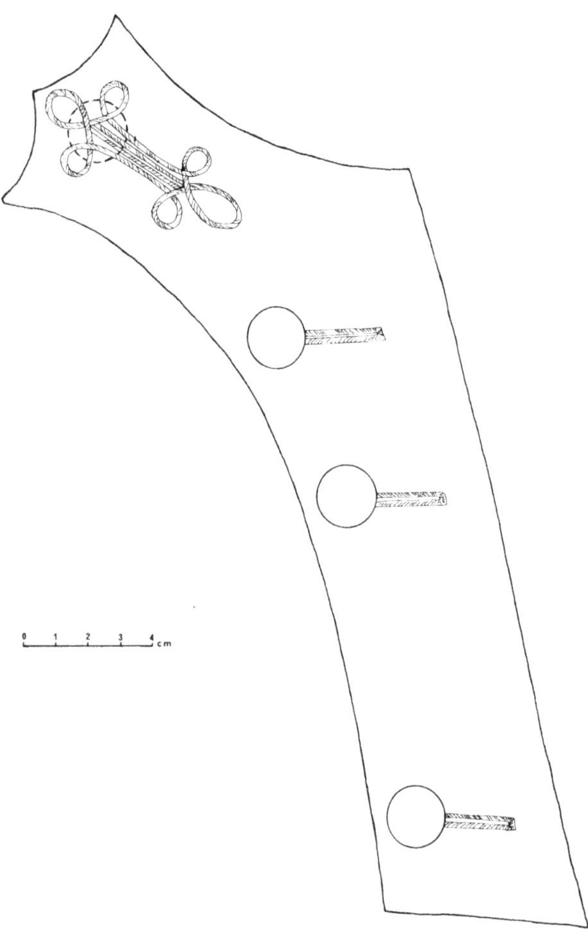

Lapel of a regimental quartermaster, 1790–99. This drawing is to scale, and shows the small size of lapels; the top button is omitted to show the embroidery clearly. The lapel, traced from the official pattern, measures 23cm from top to bottom and 6.4cm wide at the bottom; buttons were 1.9cm in diameter. (Bavarian War Archives, München)

these being in the facing colour and bearing the electoral crest in yellow. On each sleeve were four white or yellow chevrons, point up. Drums were brass with light blue and white striped hoops.

Light Infantry

In 1799 the light infantry adopted the Raupenhelm and coat as for the line infantry, but the coat was light green (this changed to dark green in 1809); the turnbacks were red, the breeches grey. The élite company had a green plume to the left side of the Raupenhelm, the other companies wore coloured tufts: 1st—white; 2nd—green; 3rd—red; 4th—blue; 5th—yellow. In 1811 Karabinier companies were raised, which wore red plumes. Lapels and cuffs were black with red piping; the collar and buttons were in the regimental colour. Regimental facings and title changes were as follows:

Year	*Titles*	*Collar*	*Buttons*
1801	'Metzen' (raised from 1st Feldjägers)	red	white, yellow from 1804
1804	1st Leichte-Infanterie-Bataillon 'Metzen'	"	"
1807	1st 'Habermann'	"	"
1809	1st 'Gedoni'	"	"
1811	1st 'Hertling' then 'Fick'	"	"
1815	1st 'Fortis'	"	"
1801	'Clossmann' (raised from 1st Feldjägers)	red	white
1804	2nd Leichte-Infanterie-Bataillon 'Vincenti'	"	"
1805	2nd 'Ditfurth'	"	"
1808	2nd 'Wreden'	"	"
1811	2nd 'Treuberg' then 'Merz'	"	"
1815	2nd 'Sebus'	"	"
1801	1st 'Salern' (raised from 2nd Feldjägers)	black, edged red	yellow, white from 1804
1804	3rd 'Preysing'	"	"
1808	3rd 'Bernclau'	"	"
1811	3rd 'Scherer'	"	"
1813	Combined with the 1st and 2nd Battalions of the Würzburg Infantry Regt. to form the new 12th Line Infantry Regt.	"	"
1801	2nd 'Salern' (raised from 2nd Feldjägers)	black edged red	yellow
1804	4th 'Stengel'	"	"
1806	4th 'Zoller'	"	"
1807	4th 'Wreden'	"	"
1809	4th 'Donnersberg'	"	"
1810	4th 'Theobald'	"	"
1813	4th 'Cronegg'	"	"
1815	Converted to 1st Battalion, 16th Line Infantry Regt.	"	"

		Facings	*Buttons*
1803	'de la Motte'	Crimson collar, lapels and cuffs until 1806 when	white
1804	5th 'de la Motte'		
1806	Absorbed the Nürnberg infantry battalion.		

Sealed pattern for the epaulette of the Rumford coat; a black leather strap edged in white cord, with a brass crescent and chain attached. In 1790 they were worn far back on the shoulder, moving forward to the crown of the shoulder later in the period. (Bavarian Army Museum)

1807 5th 'Dalwigk' 1808 5th 'Buttler' 1812 5th 'Herrmann' 1814 5th 'Treuberg' 1815 Converted to 2nd Battalion, 16th Line Infantry Regt.	lapels and cuffs became black edged red and the collar became lemon yellow, piped red.	
1803 'Lessel' 1804 6th 'Lessel' then 'Weinbach' 1806 6th 'Taxis' 1809 6th 'La Roche' 1812 6th 'Palm' 1814 6th 'Flad'. This unit was then used to form the new 14th Line Infantry Regt. together with the 1st and 2nd Battalions of the Frankfurt Infantry Regt.	Crimson collar, lapels and cuffs until 1806 when lapels and cuffs became black edged red and the collar became lemon yellow, with red edging.	yellow
1808 7th 'Günther' (newly raised)	Collar light blue edged red	white

In 1807 a Tiroler-Jäger-Bataillon was briefly raised. This wore a black shako with white loop and button, light blue and white cockade; single-breasted dark grey coat with light blue collar and cuffs both edged dark green; white buttons; grey breeches; dark green shoulder-straps edged light blue; black bandoliers.

In 1813 Freiwillige Jäger battalions were raised. They wore the shako with cockade, loop and button; short, single-breasted dark green coat with yellow collar; yellow piping to front of coat and to green cuffs, shoulder-straps and turnbacks; yellow buttons; dark green trousers with yellow side-stripes; black bandoliers; rifles.

Grenadier-Garde-Regiment

Raised 1814. Large bearskin cap in black fur with brass plate bearing the Bavarian crowned arms with lion supporters, white cords, white-over-light blue feather plume. Light blue coat with poppy red collar, lapels, cuffs, turnbacks and piping. White buttons bearing a grenade, white buttonhole lace to lapel and cuff buttons.

Sealed pattern of buttonhole lace for 1st and 2nd Line Infantry Regiments, 1799–1815. (Bavarian Army Museum)

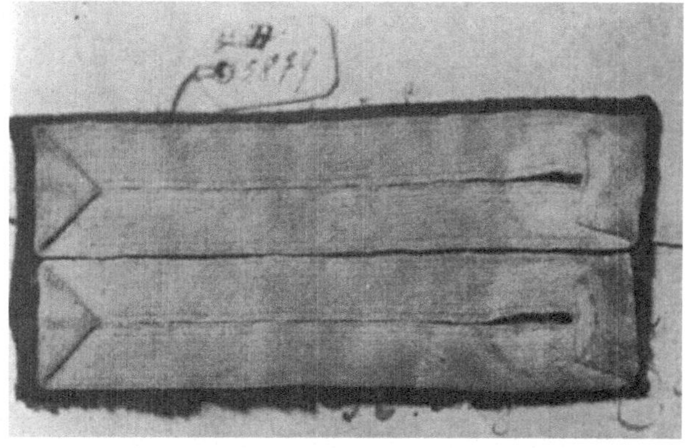

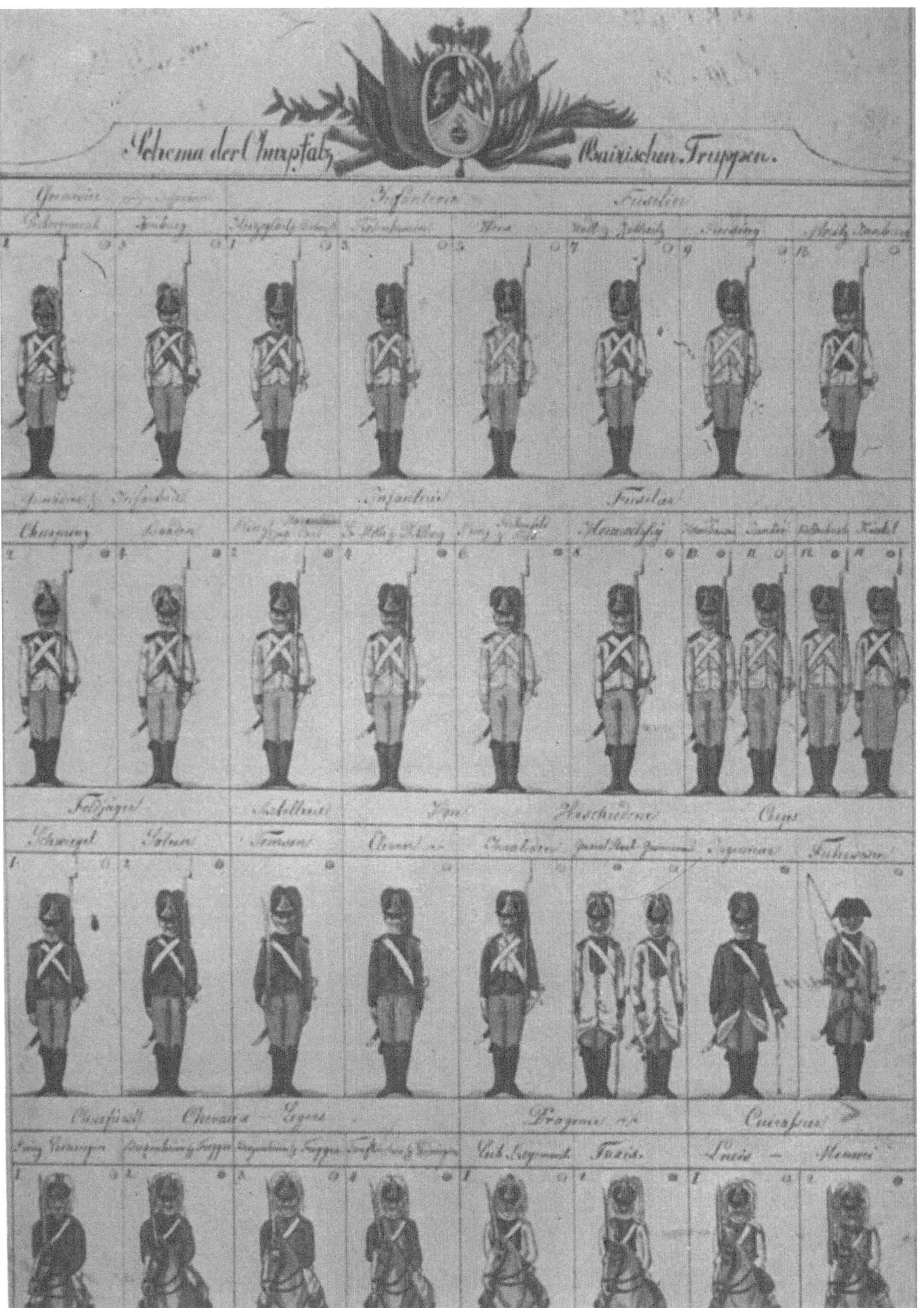
Schema der Churpfalz Bairischen Truppen.
Infanterie
Fusilier
Infanterie
Fusilier
Dragoner
Cuirassier

Narrow white piping to top and front of collar and to cuff. White bandoliers and breeches; long black gaiters with white buttons for the men, knee-boots for the officers. Off duty they wore the Raupenhelm with white-over-light blue tuft to left side and with the inscription GRENADIER-GARDE-REGIMENT on the brass front plate.

1st and 2nd Jäger Battalions
Raised 1815. Raupenhelm as for the line infantry, with inscription on the frontal band 1 tes (2 tes) JAEGER-BATAJLLON. The Karabinier companies wore green plumes, the other companies wore company tufts. The cornflower blue coat was of line infantry cut with grass green collar, lapels and cuffs, grass green piping to cuff flap and cornflower blue shoulder-straps, grass green turnbacks and brass buttons with the battalion number. Grass green breeches, short black gaiters, shoes. Black bandoliers; powder horn on green cords with green tassels. Armament was a short rifle for the Karabiniers, smooth-bore muskets for the Jägers.

The Garrison Regiment
Infantry Raupenhelm; single-breasted, dark blue, long-skirted coat with white collar, cuffs and piping, yellow buttons. Grey waistcoat and breeches, short black gaiters (boots for officers). White bandoliers; muskets. Officers wore the waist sash until 1818.

Artillery Uniforms 1799–1815

1st or Horse Artillery Battery
Cavalry Raupenhelm with red plume on left side and with ARTJLLERIE-REGIMENT on the front band; dark blue, double-breasted, short-skirted coat with scarlet collar and cuffs; black lapels and cuff flaps piped scarlet; scarlet turnbacks with yellow grenades; yellow buttons, and brass scale epaulettes on red backing. Dark blue breeches; boots and spurs. Until 1812 officers wore the sash, then the cavalry-style bandolier in silver and light blue. The sabre was in an iron sheath on black slings. Saddle furniture of dragoon pattern in dark blue edged red, with white sheepskin saddle cloth for the men, black bearskin for officers.

Chart of the Bavarian Army, 1790–99: an exhibit in the Bavarian Army Museum. At the top is the Kur-Pfalz-Bavarian crest—gold lion on black, light blue and white lozenges, gold orb on red. The regimental titles are:
***Top, l to r:* 1.Leib-Regiment; 3.Isenburg (*also* 'Ysenburg'), both Grenadiers; 1.Herzog Carl von Zweibrücken; 3.Rodenhausen; 5.Weix, 1792 (*also* 'Weichs'); 7.Wahl/Zedtwitz; 9.Preising (*also* 'Preysing'); 13.Moritz Isenburg.**
***Second row, l to r:* 2.Churprinz (*also* 'Kurprinz'); 4.Baaden, both Grenadiers; 2.Prinz Carl; 4.De la Motte; 6.Prinz von Pirkenfeld (*sic*); 8.Morawitzky; 10.Hohenhausen; 11.Junker; 12.Belderbusch; 14.Kinkel.**
***Third row, l to r:* 1.Schweigel; 2.Salern, both Feldjäger; Tomson (artillery); Eleven (cadets); Invaliden; General-Staab u. Garnison; Ingeniure; Fahrwesen (train).**
***Bottom row, l to r:* 1.Prinz Leiningen; 2.Bretzenheim; 3.Wahl/Fugger; 4. (not fully formed or titled), all Chevau-Légers; 1.Leib-Regiment; 2.Taxis, both Dragoons; 1.Louis*; 2.Minucci*, both Kürassiers. (* = does not coincide with printed records which show Minucci as 1st and Winkelhausen as 2nd.)**

2nd or Foot Batteries
As for Horse Artillery except; white belts; black gaiters with yellow buttons; heavy, straight-bladed sword with brass hilt having a lion's head pommel. Officers adopted the gorget in 1812 in place of the sash.

Train
In 1800 they wore a large round hat; grey, single-breasted tunic with light blue collar and cuffs, white buttons; grey waistcoat, and grey overalls trimmed in black leather. In 1806 they were 'militarized' (taken on to the army establishment) and their uniform was the cavalry pattern Raupenhelm with no plume or inscription on the front band; grey, single-breasted tunic, light blue collar, cuffs and edging to grey turnbacks; white buttons, white metal shoulder-scales on light blue tacking; grey breeches. Officers wore cavalry sabres on white waistbelts and until 1808 the men carried no weapons; after this they were issued with basket-hilted Prussian sabres on black bandoliers. On the upper left arm the drivers wore a blue band holding an oval brass shield bearing 'MJK'.

Cavalry Uniforms 1799–1815

The Raupenhelm was similar to the infantry pattern except that it had two brass struts passing over the crown from chinstrap boss to chinstrap boss, and on the left side was worn a large white plume. Across the helmet front band was the regimental title: CHEV-LEGERS-REGJMENT or DRAGONER-REGJMENT.

Kürassiers and dragoons wore white coats with

Raupenhelm of an officer of Chevau-Légers, 1806–15. The gilded reinforcing struts passing up the skull vertically at the side and diagonally at the rear can be seen here. The cockade and plume socket were covered with light blue and silver embroidery. The only point which differs from regulations is the form of the gilt studs holding up the centres of the two loops of chain—these are plain, and should be lion-masks for an officer. Perhaps this exhibit should be labelled as the helmet of a sergeant-major? (Bavarian Army Museum)

white collars and with facings shown on lapels, cuffs and turnback edgings. On the shoulders were white metal scale epaulettes on a backing of the facing colour. Other details were as before except that the boots were now of below-knee-length. Dragoon troopers wore a red waist sash, those of Chevau-Légers a grey sash. Chevau-Légers wore light green coats (changed to dark green in November 1809) and in the turnback corners were white electoral caps, which in 1805 became white crowns and rampant lions. Breeches and belts were white. Officers wore silver and light blue bandoliers and waist sashes.

In 1804 the last Kürassier regiment was converted to dragoons and in 1811 both dragoon regiments were converted to Chevau-Légers, making six regiments of this arm in all. Harness was black with white metal fittings. Saddle furniture was red with white and light blue diced borders, white sheepskin saddle cloth. Officers' gala horse furniture was green with golden edging and royal cypher and black sheepskin.

1 1790 1st Kürassier-Regt. 'Minucci'—scarlet facings, white buttons.
1804 1st Dragoner-Regt. 'Minucci'—collar now scarlet instead of white.
1811 1st Chevau-Légers-Regt.—scarlet facings, white buttons.

2 1790 2nd Kürassier-Regt. 'Winckelhausen'—scarlet facings, yellow buttons.
1799 Converted to 4th Chevau-Légers-Regt. and then to 1st Chevau-Légers-Regt. 'Kurfürst'. Light green coat, collar now poppy red, poppy red facings, white buttons.
1804 2nd Chevau-Légers-Regt. 'Kurfürst'.
1806 2nd Chevau-Légers-Regt. 'König'.
1811 4th Chevau-Légers-Regt. 'König'.

3 1790 1st Dragoner-Regt. 'Leibdragoner'—black facings, white buttons.
1801 1st Dragoner-Regt.
1803 Disbanded.

4 1790 2nd Dragoner-Regt. 'Taxis'—black facings (white collar), yellow buttons.
1803 Scarlet facings and collar.
1806 Absorbed the Nürnberg cavalry and the Prussian Husaren-Bataillon 'von Bila'.
1811 Converted to 2nd Chevau-Légers-Regt. 'Taxis'—facings changed to red.

5 1790 1st Chevau-Légers-Regt. 'Prinz Leiningen'—black facings, white buttons.
1799 4th Chevau-Légers-Regt. 'Prinz Leiningen'—yellow buttons.
1803 3rd Chevau-Légers-Regt. 'Prinz Leiningen'.
1811 5th Chevau-Légers-Regt. 'Prinz Leiningen'—poppy red facings from

1806, yellow buttons.

6 1790 2nd Chevau-Légers-Regt. 'La Rosée'—black facings, yellow buttons.

1799 3rd Chevau-Légers-Regt. 'vacant Fürst Bretzenheim'.

1801 Disbanded.

7 1790 3rd Chevau-Légers-Regt. 'Wahl'—apple green facings, white buttons.

1799 2nd Chevau-Légers-Regt. 'Fugger'.

1804 1st Chevau-Légers-Regt. 'Kurprinz'.

1806 1st Chevau-Légers-Regt. 'Kronprinz'—black facings and collar with red edging, yellow buttons.

1811 3rd Chevau-Légers-Regt. 'Kronprinz'.

8 1803 4th Chevau-Légers-Regt. 'Bubenhofen' (newly raised from Würzburg cavalry)—black facings (and collar) edged red, white buttons.

1811 6th Chevau-Légers-Regt. 'Bubenhofen'.

9 1813 National-Chevau-Légers-Regt. (then 7th Chevau-Légers-Regt. 'Prinz Karl von Bayern')—poppy red facings, white buttons; shako with cockade, white loop and button over crowned brass plate bearing 'MJK', white cords and plume (green plume for skirmishers). Officers and NCOs had silver top bands to their shakos.

Lancers

Raised 1813. Their uniform was copied from that of the Austrian Uhlans and initially consisted of a yellow-topped *czapka* with white piping and cords, white plume; dark green *kurtka* with light blue collar, lapels, cuffs, turnbacks and piping; white buttons; dark green breeches with double light blue side-stripes. On the shoulders were white metal scale epaulettes, and the waist sash was white and light blue. Saddle furniture was red with white edging, harness black with white metal fittings. The lance had a white-over-light blue pennant. Trumpeters had red plumes and their facings (collar, cuffs and lapels) were edged in silver. They had silver fringes to their epaulettes and light blue (later red) 'wings' on the rear of the jacket. In 1814 all light blue facings were replaced by poppy red and the buttons became yellow.

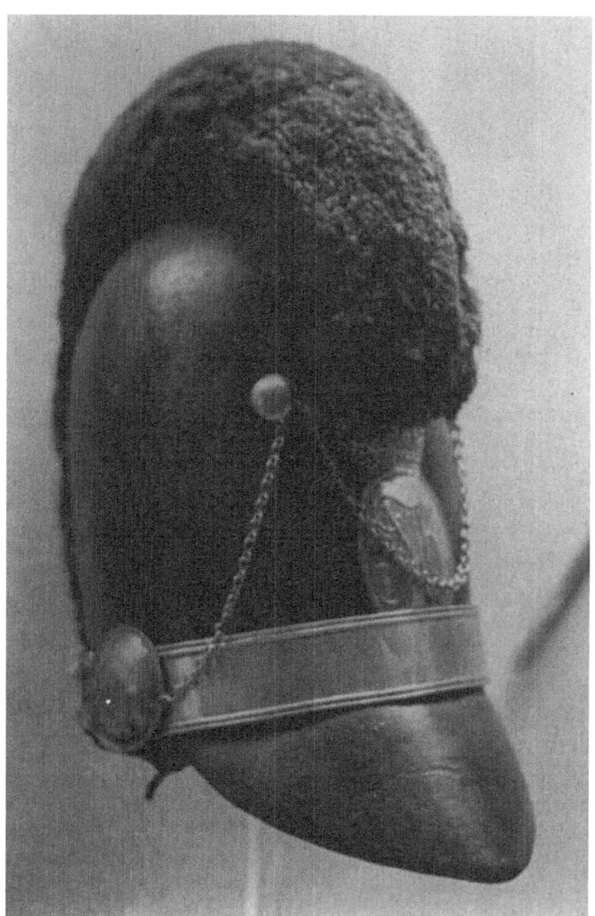

Raupenhelm of an infantry fusilier private, 1806–15. The crowned oval plate with the 'MJK' cypher has slipped a little behind the brass front band; the brass-edged chinstrap is almost invisible, buckled horizontally round the rear part of the band. This incredibly awkward leather helmet with a 'stuffed sausage' crest was over 30cm high, and represented an extreme sartorial backlash by Bavarian traditionalists against Rumford's utilitarian reforms. It was so tall that NCOs kept their notebooks inside the crown, and there was even a serious suggestion that the mess-tin should be designed to fit inside it. (Bavarian Army Museum)

1st and 2nd Kürassiers

Raised 1815. Steel helmet with combe and black sheepskin crest for the men, black bearskin for officers, NCOs and trumpeters; cornflower blue tunic with poppy red collar, lapels and cuffs all piped light blue; white breeches; high, cuffed boots with buckle-on spurs. French-style cuirasses in steel with brass shoulder-straps; white metal epaulettes, white gauntlets. French saddle with black sheepskin edged red, red saddle furniture edged white, white crowned 'MJK' in the rear

Front and rear views of a Chevau-Légers tunic, 1815. Facings are poppy red, the buttons plain brass. Note white turnback ornaments. (Bavarian Army Museum)

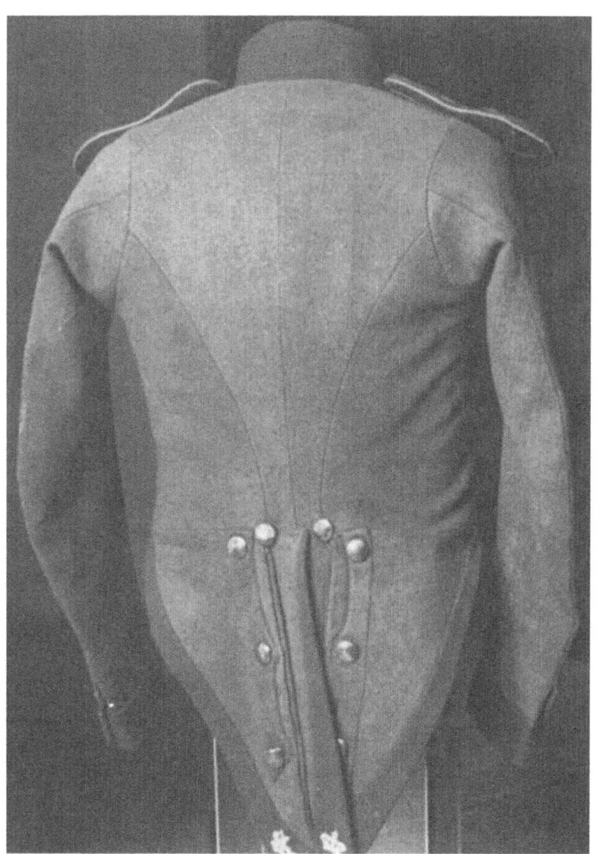

corners; black harness with white fittings. Armament was the carbine, pistols and Pallasch. Trumpeters had brass helmets with red crests (light blue for gala wear), no cuirass, and red 'wings' on the gala tunic.

1st and 2nd Hussars

Raised 1815. Shako (black for the 1st Regiment, red for the 2nd) with white-over-light blue plume, white and light blue pompon, white loop and button, white cords; light blue dolman, pelisse and breeches, white buttons and lace, black fur; white and light blue barrel sash; white bandoliers, black sabretache with white metal crowned 'MJK'. Brass-hilted sabre in steel sheath. Black harness with white fittings, red saddle furniture edged white with white crowned 'MJK' badge in rear corners. Plain black hussar boots. Trumpeters had apple green shakos with red plumes and gold cords; red dolman, pelisse and breeches with gold buttons and lace; red sabretache with gold embroidery and edging; light blue saddle furniture edged gold. Badges of rank took the form of white (silver for officers) chevrons over the cuffs and white/silver embroidery around the thigh knots. Troopers wore tufts at the bases of their plumes in the squadron colours: 1st—white; 2nd—green; 3rd—red; 4th—blue; 5th—yellow; 6th—red and black; 7th—green and black.

Garde du Corps

Raised 16 July 1814. Brass helmet and combe with black bearskin crest and brown sealskin turban and peak; cornflower blue frock coat with poppy red collar, lapels, cuffs and turnbacks (the latter with white crown badges in the corners). White guard's lace to collar and cuffs; white gauntlets and breeches; white buttons and epaulettes. Steel cuirass covered in brass with brass shoulder-chains on red cloth; red 'cuff' edged white. High, cuffed boots with buckle-on spurs, Pallasch in steel sheath. Black harness with white fittings, white sheepskin saddle cover, red saddle furniture with white edging and crowned 'MJK'. Trumpeters had red helmet crests with the blue uniform; for gala wear they had red tunics faced light blue and light blue helmet crests. Their uniforms were trimmed in silver lace.

Landhusarenkorps

Raised October 1813. As for the 1st Hussars except: white pelisse with black lambskin trim, black bandolier and belts. Officers had (from 1814) red saddle furniture edged silver. The barrel sash was light blue and white in six rows. *Freiwilliges Husarenregiment* Raised May 1814 from the Landhusaren. As for 1st Hussars.

Bavarian Landwehr (National II Klasse)

At the battle of Hanau, 29–31 October 1813, they are known to have worn: black felt shako, blue and white cockade, white loop and button. On the top of the cockade, the company tuft (green plume for sharpshooters); at top left of the shako was a battalion badge in rosette form—red, white, blue and yellow for 1st, 2nd, 3rd and 4th

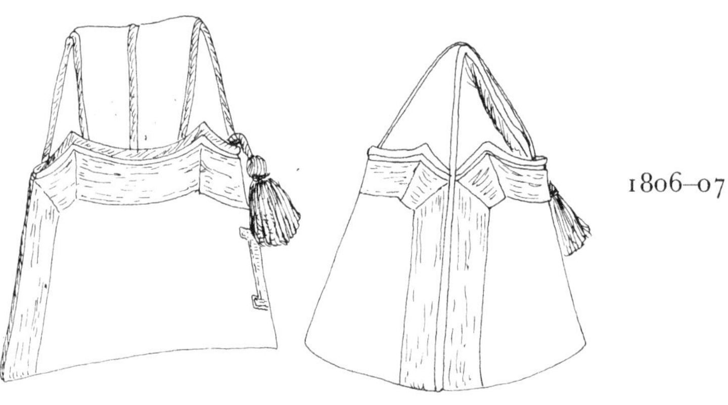

The *Holzmütze*—fatigue cap—of 1799–1815. Made of coat-colour cloth, this was piped in facing colour, and bore a company badge on the front of the band; a red grenade for Grenadiers, and for Füsiliers the initial letter of the company title in the button colour, on a shield of facing colour.

respectively. Coat as for line infantry but single-breasted, with poppy red collar, cuffs and turnbacks; nine white buttons on the front. Long cornflower blue trousers worn over short black gaiters; white bandoliers; plain black pouch; sabres for NCOs only. No sash worn by officers.

Bavarian Combat Involvement and Orders of Battle 1800-15

Summary:

1800 Bavaria joined with Austria against France; Bavaria was invaded and the Imperial forces (under Erzherzog Johann) were defeated by Moreau at the battle of Hohenlinden on 3 December 1800. Bavaria transferred to the French camp.

1805 The Austrians under General Mack invaded Bavaria and Württemberg and occupied Ulm. Napoleon, with his Bavarian allies, outflanked Mack and bottled him up in Ulm, causing his shameful capitulation there on 14–15 October 1805.

1806–07 The Bavarian contingent took part in the sieges of the following Prussian fortresses, which surrendered on the dates shown: Plassenburg and Grossglogau (1 December 1806), Breslau (5 January 1807), Brieg (16 January 1807), Kosel (held out until the end of the war), Glatz (24 January 1807) and Neisse (1 June 1807).

1809 The Bavarians formed the VIII Corps of the Grande Armée; they fought at Abensberg (20 April), Echmuhl (22 April), Regensburg (23 April), Aspern-Essling (21–22 May) and Wagram (4–6 July). In addition to this the newly acquired province of Tyrol (1805) rose in revolt three Tyrol (1805) rose in revolt three times against Bavaria, and was not finally pacified until mid-October 1809, and then only by the efforts of the whole Bavarian army. During the revolts many French formations and their German allies (Ducal Saxons, for example) were destroyed by the Tyrolean rebels.

1812 The Bavarian army formed the VI Corps of the Grande Armée and became north flank guard at Polozk, where they fought two large battles (16–18 August and 18–20 October). The six Chevau-Léger regiments were taken from the Corps by Napoleon early in the campaign and went with the main body of the army to Moscow, being largely destroyed at the battle of Borodino (6–7 September). About 80 per cent of the Bavarian army was lost in Russia, including all the flags which entered that country.

1813 The newly reconstituted Bavarian army was again the VI Corps in the campaign in Saxony up to the armistice. They then abandoned

The Bavarian Army at Hohenlinden
3 December 1800

(First figures in each group are starting strengths; losses in brackets.)
Commander: Generallieutenant Freiherr von Zweibrücken

Unit	Officers	Other ranks	Totals	Horses
1st Brigade (Bavarian): Generalmajor von Deroy				
Combined Chevau-Légers-Regt.	50 (1)	911 (17)	961 (18)	888 (69)
Fussjäger-Div. Kessling	7 (3)	289 (182)	296 (185)	–
Grenadier-Bn. Reuss	16 (10)	593 (193)	609 (203)	–
Feldjäger-Bn. Metzen	20 (7)	593 (192)	613 (199)	–
Füsilier-Bn. Minucci	20 (9)	597 (198)	617 (207)	–
Füsilier-Bn. Stengel	16 (–)	703 (96)	719 (96)	–
Füsilier-Bn. Sprety	15 (–)	577 (–)	592 (–)	–
Füsilier-Bn. Schlossberg	17 (6)	744 (148)	761 (166)	–
2nd Brigade (Pfalzischen): Oberst von Wrede				
Grenadier-Bn. Pompey	16 (–)	688 (188)	704 (188)	–
Feldjäger-Bn. Preysing	16 (2)	589 (176)	605 (178)	–
Füsilier-Bn. Busseck	16 (7)	718 (176)	734 (183)	–
Füsilier-Bn. Dalwigk	16 (1)	696 (30)	716 (31)	–
Füsilier-Bn. Zoller	16 (–)	604 (30)	620 (30)	–
Füsilier-Bn. de la Motte	15 (–)	677 (14)	682 (14)	–
Totals:	256 (46)	8,969 (1,640)	9,229 (1,698)	888 (69)
Of these, killed in action	3	21	24	32
Wounded	7	83	90	30
Captured/missing	36	1,544	1,580	7

Artillery
Start strength was 32 guns in one horse artillery and three and a half foot artillery companies (batteries); of these, five cannon, 13 howitzers, four Wurst and six horse artillery guns were lost—a total of 28 pieces.
Percentage Losses of Strengths Engaged
18.4% of men; 7.8% of horses; 94% of guns.

Napoleon and joined Prussia, Russia and Austria against him at Leipzig; and later at Hanau (30–31 October), where they were beaten by the French.

1814 The campaign in France; sieges of Hüningen (near Basle), Belfort and Schlettstadt; the clashes of Rosnay, Louisetaines, Bray, Villeneuve and Vendreuvres; the battles of Brienne (29 January), Bar sur Aube (24 January), Arcis sur Aube (20 March).

1815 Invasion of central France—very little action.

Bavarian Order of Battle 1806–07

1st Army Division: Generallieutenant von Deroy
1st Brigade: Generalmajor von Siebein
1st Infanterie-Regt.
10th Infanterie-Regt.
6th Light Bn.
1st Chevau-Légers-Regt.
One 6pdr. artillery battery
2nd Brigade: Generalmajor von Raglovich
4th Infanterie-Regt.
5th Infanterie-Regt.
Fussjäger Division
1st Dragoner-Regt.
One 6pdr. artillery battery

2nd Army Division: Generallieutenant von Wrede
1st Brigade: Generalmajor Graf Mezanelli
2nd Infanterie-Regt.
13th Infanterie-Regt.
3rd Light Bn.
2nd Chevau-Légers-Regt.
One 6pdr. artillery battery
2nd Brigade: Generalmajor Franz Graf Minucci
3rd Infanterie-Regt.
7th Infanterie-Regt.
4th Light Bn.
3rd Chevau-Légers-Regt.
One 6pdr. battery

Raupenhelm of an officer, 1st Jäger Bn., 1815; and in the background the cornflower blue and silver fatigue cap—*Holzmütze*—of an infantry officer. (Bavarian Army Museum)

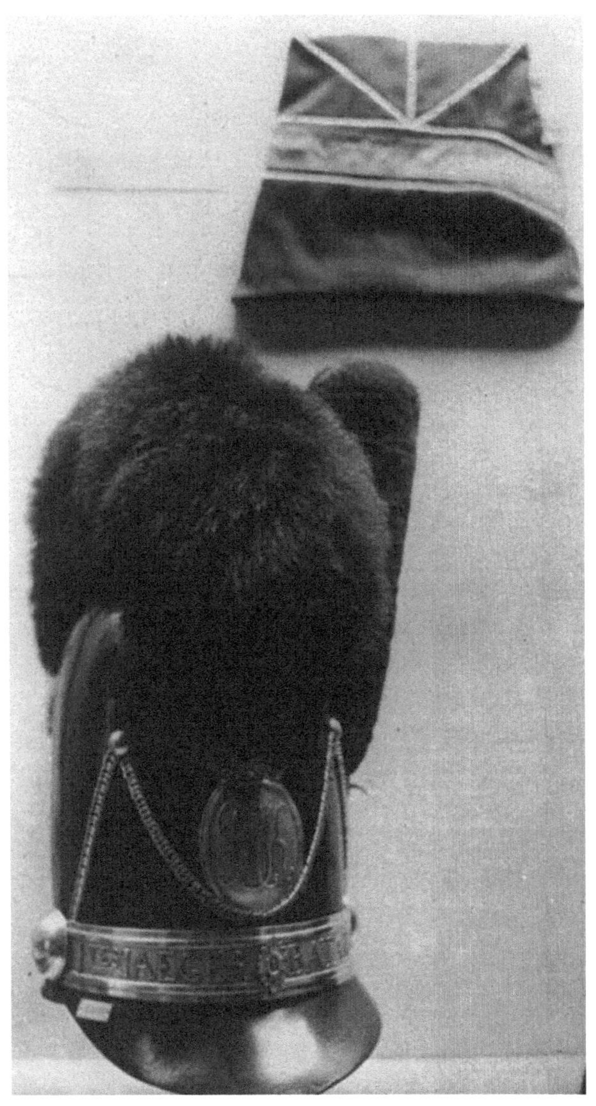

Reserve Division: Generallieutenant Graf Ysenburg
1st Brigade: Generalmajor Graf Marsigli
8th Infanterie-Regt.
9th Infanterie-Regt.
5th Light Bn.
4th Chevau-Légers-Regt.
One 12pdr. battery
2nd Brigade: Generallieutenant von Kinkel
6th Infanterie-Regt.
11th Infanterie-Regt.
2nd Light Bn.
2nd Dragoner-Regt.
One 6pdr. battery
Artillery Reserve
One Fahrende battery
One 6pdr. battery
One 12pdr. battery
Artillery park

Bavarian Order of Battle 1809 (at the start of operations)

Commander: Marshal Lefebvre, Duke of Danzig

1st Division: Generallieutenant Kronprinz Ludwig
1st Brigade: Generalmajor von Rechberg
1st Infanterie-Regt.
2nd Infanterie-Regt. 'Kronprinz'
1st Light Bn.
2nd Brigade: Generalmajor von Stengel (9 bns.)
4th Infanterie-Regt. 'vacant Salern'
8th Infanterie-Regt. 'Herzog Pius'
3rd Light Bn. 'Bernclau' (detached in Tyrol)
Cavalry Brigade: Generalmajor Baron Zandt (6½ sqns.)
1st Dragoner-Regt. 'vacant von Minucci' (two sqns. detached in Tyrol)
1st Chevau-Légers-Regt. 'Kronprinz'
Artillery (8,678 men)
2 line batteries—6 guns each
1 light battery—6 guns

2nd Division: Generallieutenant Baron Wrede
1st Brigade: Generalmajor Graf Minucci
3rd Infanterie-Regt. 'Prinz Karl'
13th Infanterie-Regt.
6th Light Bn. 'La Roche'
2nd Brigade: Generalmajor Graf Beckers (9 bns.)

Trooper, Chevau-Légers Regt. 'Fugger', 1792

1. Captain, 5th Füsilier-Regt. 'von Wahl', 1792–99
2. Colonel, 1st Feldjäger-Regt. 'von Schweicheldt', 1792–99
3. Drum-Major, 1st Füsilier-Regt., 1790–99

B

1. Captain, Horse Artillery, 1801–04
2. Füsilier Drummer, 2nd Line Infantry Regt. 'Kronprinz', 1807
3. Grenadier, 4th Line Infantry Regt. 'Salern', 1806

Trooper, 1st Dragoons, 1807

D

1. 1st Lieutenant, 14th Line Infantry Regt., 1809
2. Sergeant-Major, 2nd Chevau-Légers Regt. 'König', 1809
3. Corporal, 3rd Füsilier Company, 11th Line Infantry Regt. 'Kinkel', 1810

E

1. Private, 4th Light Infantry Bn. 'Theobald', 1812
2. 2nd Lieutenant, 1st Chevau-Légers Regt. 'Kronprinz', 1809
3. Captain, 1st Dragoons, 1806–11

F

1. 2nd Lieutenant, Grenadier-Garde, 1815
2. 2nd Lieutenant, Uhlanen-Regt., 1813
3. Lieutenant-Colonel, 1st Kürassier-Regt. 'Prinz Karl', 1815

Trumpeter, 1st Bavarian Hussars, 1815

H

6th Infanterie-Regt. 'Herzog Wilhelm'
7th Infanterie-Regt. 'Löwenstein'
4th Light Bn. 'Donnersberg' (detached in Tyrol)
Cavalry Brigade: Generalmajor Graf Preysing (8½ sqns.)
2nd Chevau-Légers-Regt. 'König'
3rd Chevau-Légers-Regt. 'Leiningen'
Artillery (8,938 men)
2 line batteries—6 guns each
1 light battery—6 guns

(Wrede's Division was present at the battle of Wagram on 6 July 1809. After Macdonald's massed assault had failed to break the Austrian centre, Napoleon ordered Wrede to take over and to attack again at the same point. By skilful use of his artillery in a mobile fire-and-movement rôle, Wrede broke the already weakened Austrian line without having to commit his infantry or cavalry to close combat. He was wounded by a cannon-ball, and when Napoleon was informed that General Minucci was to take over in his place he said: 'As long as he carries on as Wrede has started he will do well.' In the subsequent pursuit of the beaten Austrian army the Bavarians fought at Staatz on 9 July; at Tesswitz on the 10th, where they lost 850 men; and at Znaim on 11 July.)

3rd Division: Generallieutenant von Deroy
1st Brigade: Generalmajor von Vincenti
9th Infanterie-Regt. 'Ysenburg'
10th Infanterie-Regt. 'Junker'
5th Light Bn. 'Buttler'
2nd Brigade: Generalmajor von Siebein (10 bns.)
5th Infanterie-Regt. 'Preysing'
14th Infanterie-Regt.
7th Light Bn. 'Günther'
Cavalry Brigade: Generalmajor Graf Seydewitz (8½ sqns.)
2nd Dragoner-Regt. 'Taxis'
4th Chevau-Légers-Regt. 'Bubenhofen'
Artillery (9,947 men)
2 line batteries—6 guns each
1 light battery —6 guns
Corps Artillery Reserve
18 guns and 388 men
Total: 28,065 men

In the Tyrol under Generallieutenant Freiherr von Kinkel were:

11th Infanterie-Regt. 'Kinkel'	—10 companies
2nd Light Bn. 'Wreden'	—4 companies
3rd Light Bn. 'Bernclau'	—4 companies
4th Light Bn. 'Donnersberg'	—4 companies
1st Dragoner-Regt.	—2 squadrons

Bavarian Order of Battle 1812 (at the start of operations)

VI Corps of the Grande Armée

Commander: Colonel-General of Cuirassiers Count Gouvion St Cyr
Chief of General Staff: Colonel d'Albignac
Commander of Artillery: Colonel de Colonge

19th Infantry Division

Commander: General von Deroy (killed at Polozk, 10 August 1812)
Staff Officer: Major von Gravenreuth
1st Infantry Brigade: Generalmajor von Siebein (3,697 men)
1st Light Bn.
1st Infanterie-Leib-Regt. (2 bns.)
9th Infanterie-Regt. 'Ysenburg'
2nd Infantry Brigade: Generalmajor von Raglovich (3,757 men)
3rd Light Bn.
4th Infanterie-Regt. 'Sachsen-Hildburghausen'
10th Infanterie-Regt. 'Junker'
3rd Infantry Brigade: Generalmajor Graf Richberg (3,404 men)
6th Light Bn.
8th Infanterie-Regt. 'Herzog Pius'
13th Infanterie-Regt. (vacant)*
1st Cavalry Brigade (later, 20th Light Cavalry Bde.): Generalmajor Graf Seydewitz (1,522 men, 1,654 horses)
1st Chevau-Légers-Regt. (4 sqns.)**
3rd Chevau-Légers-Regt. 'Kronprinz' (4 sqns.)***
6th Chevau-Légers-Regt. 'Bubenhofen' (4 sqns.)***
Artillery Detachment: Oberst Freiherr von Lamey

1st Light Bty.*** 3rd Light Bty.	Each of four 6pdr. guns and two 7pdr. howitzers, each with six-horse team.
1st Line Bty. 2nd Line Bty.*	Each of four 6pdr. guns and two 7pdr. howitzers, each with four-horse team.
6th Line Bty.	12pdrs., six-horse team.

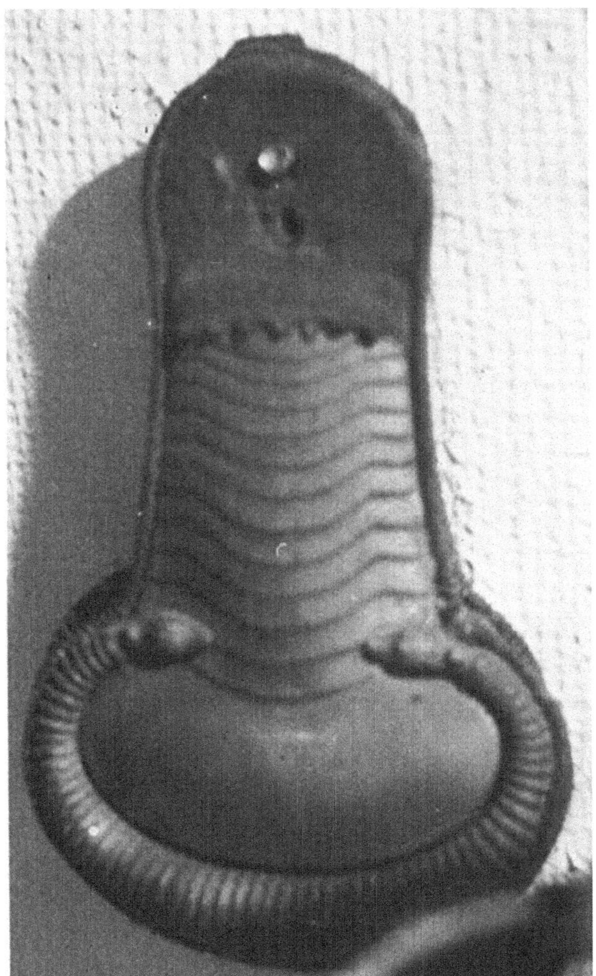

White metal shoulder-scale of a Chevau-Légers cavalryman, 1800–15. The elaborate metal parts were sewn onto a padded red cloth backing, and the button—missing from this example—rested on a red cloth upper section. (Heimat-Museum, Sonthofen)

Notes

* Detached in Danzig; later attached to X Corps (Macdonald)

** Detached 27 March to 3rd Light Cavalry Division (Chastel) of III Cavalry Corps (Grouchy) to form 17th Light Cavalry Bde. under French General Domanget, together with Saxon Chevau-Légers-Regt. 'Prinz Clemens'.

*** Detached 14 July by Napoleon's command, to join Advanced Guard as 'Preysing's Cavalry Division'.

20th Infantry Division

Commander: General der Kavallerie Graf von Wrede

Staff Officer: Oberst von Comeau

1st Infantry Brigade: Generalmajor von Vincenti (3,849 men)

2nd Light Bn.

2nd Infanterie-Regt. 'Kronprinz' (2 bns.)

6th Infanterie-Regt. 'Herzog Wilhelm' (2 bns.)

2nd Infantry Brigade: Generalmajor Graf Beckers (3,814 men)

4th Light Bn.

3rd Infanterie-Regt. 'Prinz Karl' (2 bns.)

7th Infanterie-Regt. 'Löwenstein-Wertheim' (2 bns.)

3rd Infantry Brigade: Generalmajor Graf Minucci (3,583 men)

5th Light Bn.

5th Infanterie-Regt. 'Preysing' (2 bns.)

11th Infanterie-Regt. 'Kinkel' (2 bns.)

2nd Cavalry Brigade (later, 21st Light Cavalry Bde.): Generalmajor von Preysing (1,439 men, 1,557 horses)

2nd Chevau-Légers-Regt. 'Taxis' (4 sqns.)**

4th Chevau-Légers-Regt. 'König' (4 sqns.)***

5th Chevau-Légers-Regt. 'Leiningen' (4 sqns.)***

(See notes under 1st Cavalry Bde. for key to asterisks.)

Artillery Detachment: Oberstlieutenant von Lamy

2nd Light Bty.
4th Light Bty.
4th Line Bty. (12 pdrs.)
5th Line Bty.
8th Line Bty.
} Composition as 19th Div. artillert, see above.

(Readers may be interested to note that the whole Bavarian artillery in 1812, with a strength of 60 guns, 24 limbers, and 451 wagons of various kinds (later, 553, after the addition of 102 bread wagons) required a total of 2,050 (later, 2,254) horses to move them.

Itinerary of the Bavarian Army in Russia, 1812

The VI Corps

2 July	Crossed the Niemen at Gogi near Prenyo (strength 30,000 infantry and 2,000 cavalry).
14 July	Wilna—reviewed by Napoleon (strength 25,000 infantry and 1,800 cavalry).

15 July	3rd, 4th, 5th, 6th Chevau-Légers and one light battery detached (see Preysing's Cavalry Division below).
29 July–4 Aug	Beschenkowitschi and area.
7 Aug	Polozk (strength 12,500 men).
16 Aug	Polozk (strength 11,000 infantry and 1,000 horses).
17–18 Aug	*First battle of Polozk* VI Corps losses 15 officers and 129 men killed; 103 officers and 1,032 men wounded; 715 men missing.
29 Aug	VI Corps strength 6,800 men.
21 Sept	All flags handed in to the commissary for safe keeping.
25 Sept	Reinforcements received; 17 officers and 321 men (300 men had died on the march from Bavaria).
18 Oct	VI Corps strength 5,000 men.
18–20 Oct	*Second battle of Polozk* II and VI Corps losses 8,000 men; retreat from Polozk begins.
24 Oct	All Bavarian flags captured at Kublitschi.
25 Oct	Globukoje—8 Bavarian guns captured.
29 Oct–13 Nov	Danilowitschi (VI Corps strength on 29 October, 2,000 men; rejoined convalescents, stragglers and detachments raised thus to 3,500 men and 24 cannon by 13 November). The first snow fell on 5 November.
19–21 Nov	Globukoje.
21–29 Nov	Dogschitzi.
1 Dec	Wilieka.
4 Dec	*Clash at Wilieka.*
5 Dec	Crossing of the Wop.
8 Dec	15 Bavarian cannon under Zoller abandoned on the hill of Ponari.
9 Dec	Berthier orders Wrede's VI Corps to become rearguard; VI Corps enters Wilna.
10 Dec	Last 12 Bavarian cannon abandoned on the hill of Ponari; VI Corps strength 300 infantry and 30 cavalry.
11 Dec	*Clash at Zizmory.*
13 Dec	VI Corps recrossed the Niemen—strength 68 men.

Preysing's Cavalry Division (21st and 22nd Light Cavalry Brigades)

15 July	Detached from VI Corps in Wilna.
19 July	Kutentsch.
22 July	Bjabez—placed under command IV Corps (Prince Eugene).
24 July	Crossed the Dwina at Beschenkowitschi.
25 July	Placed under command II Cavalry Corps (Montbrun).
1 Aug	Porjetsche.
9 Aug	Suray.
11 Aug	Welekowitschi.
15 Aug	Liady (crossed the Dnepr).

Raupenhelm helmet plate, 1806–15, bearing the 'MJK' cypher (Maximilian Joseph König); from 1799 to 1806 the cypher was 'MJ' beneath an electoral cap. (Heimat-Museum, Sonthofen)

Grenadier, 5th Infanterie-Regt. 'Preysing', 1807—a contemporary plate by Weiland which fails to show the correct proportions of the helmet, and is also wrong as to cuff detail. Facings are pink, buttons white, shoulder-straps cornflower blue with red edging, and turnbacks and plume red.

16 Aug	Krasnoi (strength 2,238 men, 2,154 horses including the artillery battery).
20 Aug	Smolensk.
25 Aug	Crossed the Wop at Pologi.
26 Aug	Dorogobusch.
29 Aug	Wiasma (met with 1st and 2nd Chevau-Légers in Grouchy's III Cavalry Corps; see below).
1 Sept	Baskakowo and Gjatz (16 men killed, 60 wounded, 50 horses killed and wounded).
7 Sept	*Battle of Borodino* (5 officers, 100 men and 100 horses killed and wounded).
9 Sept	Crossed the Moskwa and reached Ruza.
12 Sept	Zwenighorod.
15 Sept	Moscow; marched around the city to the north and bivouacked at Petrowskoje.
17 Sept	Alexiskoje (strength 800 mounted men).
22 Sept	Bezowko.
26 Sept	Perchuschkino (towards Mosaisk).
15 Oct	3rd and 6th Regiments detached to General Ornano's Division.
24 Oct	*Battle of Malojaroslawetz.*
28 Oct	Borowsk.
1 Nov	Widnmann's battery sent back to VI Corps artillery park due to lack of ammunition; captured on 9 November at the crossing of the Wop.
3 Nov	*Battle of Wiasma* Only 60 mounted officers and men of the four Bavarian regiments survived; no further concerted action took place—Preysing's Division ceased to exist.

The 1st and 2nd Chevau-Légers as part of the 3rd Light Cavalry Brigade (General Domanget) of the III Cavalry Corps (Grouchy)

17 April	Posen, as 17th Light Cavalry Brigade with the 1st Saxon Chevau-Légers.
1 June	Crossed the Vistula at Wroclawek.
25 June	Crossed the Niemen at Kowno.
28 June	Wilna.
8–12 July	Minsk.
16 July	Crossed the Beresina at Borissow.
14 Aug	Crossed the Dnepr at Chomini (clashed with Cossacks at Liady); reached Krasnoi; clashed with Cossacks.
16 Aug	*Battle of Smolensk* Losses of 1st and 2nd Regiments, 8 dead and 14 wounded.

23 Aug	Duchovtschina.
26 Aug	Dorogobusch.
29 Aug	Wiasma—met with Preysing's Cavalry Division.
1 Sept	Gjatz.
7 Sept	*Battle of Borodino* Only 180 men of both regiments fit for duty on the next day.
14 Sept	Moscow; marched through the city and out on the road to Wladimir.
21 Sept	Podolsk (1st and 2nd Regiments now only 80 men strong; the Saxon regiment numbered 50 men).
1 Oct	Tarutino.
18 Oct	*Clash at Winkowo* Losses of 1st and 2nd Regiments—66 men; only 14 remained. Regiments ceased to exist.

13th Infantry Regiment in X Corps

In April 1811 the 13th Infantry Regiment and the 2nd Artillery Battery entered Danzig to strengthen the garrison of that free city; together with the Saxon Regiment 'von Rechten' and the 7th Württemberg Infantry Regiment it became the 'German Brigade' of General Grandjean's 7th Infantry Division.

On 14 June 1812 this division moved out to Ponewiesch, and then to Bausk (18 July). They then marched to Dunaburg where they stayed until mid-September. The condition of the men was good, their losses slight. On 16 December they had withdrawn to Bausk, and on the 26th they recrossed the Niemen. Total losses were: 12 dead, 82 wounded, 114 missing and 443 sick. The six guns of this battery were the only Bavarian cannon to survive this catastrophic campaign.

Losses

In the campaign of 1812 Bavaria lost over 28,000 men; all 5,800 cavalry and train horses, all but six of her cannon; 22 flags; 260 ammunition wagons, and 300 other vehicles.

Bavarian Order of Battle at Hanau, 29–31 October 1813

2nd Division: Generallieutenant Graf Beckers
1st Brigade: Generalmajor Graf Pappenheim
4th Infanterie-Regt.
2nd Bn., Salzachkreis Landwehr
1st Bn., Regenkreis Landwehr
Combined 4th Light Bn.
Losses: 72 dead, 285 wounded, 316 missing; total, 673.
2nd Brigade: Generalmajor Freiherr von Zoller
6th Infanterie-Regt.
1st Bn., Rezatkreis Landwehr
1st Light Bn.

Private, élite company, 1st Light Infantry Bn. 'Gedoni', 1809. The tall green plume was the badge of the élite company, who were armed with rifles. Regulation lapels and cuffs were black, piped red, so the red cuffs on this Weiland plate are suspect. Buttons and helmet fittings are brass, the breeches grey; the coat changed from light to dark green in 1809.

Losses: 38 dead, 298 wounded, 258 missing; total, 594.

3rd Division: Generallieutenant de la Motte
1st Brigade: Generalmajor von Habermann
1st Bn., 7th Infanterie-Regt.
1st Bn., Unterdonaukreis Landwehr
1st Bn., Illerkreis Landwehr
1st and 2nd Bns., 11th Infanterie-Regt.
Losses: 109 dead, 199 wounded, 334 missing; total, 642.

Lieutenant, 6th Chevau-Légers-Regt. 'Bubenhofen', 1811. Dark green coat with white buttons, white metal shoulder-scales on black backing, and black facings piped red. The bandolier is striped light blue and silver and edged red, with gilt picker equipment. Another contemporary plate by Weiland.

2nd Brigade: Generalmajor von Deroy
(Not to be confused with other general of same name, killed 1812)
1st Bn., 8th Infanterie-Regt.
1st Bn., Isarkreis Landwehr
1st Bn., 9th Infanterie-Regt.
2nd Bn., Illerkreis Landwehr
1st Bn., 5th Infanterie-Regt.
Losses: 18 dead, 246 wounded, 383 missing; total, 647.

1st Cavalry Brigade: Generalmajor von Vieregg
1st Chevau-Légers-Regt.
2nd Chevau-Légers-Regt.
7th Chevau-Légers-Regt.
Losses: 21 dead, 64 wounded, 68 missing; total, 153, plus 178 horses.
2nd Cavalry Brigade: Generalmajor von Elbrach
3rd Chevau-Légers-Regt.
6th Chevau-Légers-Regt.
Losses: 9 dead, 23 wounded, 21 missing; total, 53, plus 63 horses.
3rd Cavalry Brigade: Oberst Diez
4th Chevau-Légers-Regt.
5th Chevau-Légers-Regt.
Losses: 16 dead, 40 wounded, 34 missing; total, 90, plus 89 horses.

Bavarian Colours and Standards

Records concerning this period are far from complete, and many uncertainties will probably never be resolved. The following patterns of infantry colours are recorded, and it is known that the flags lost in Russia in 1812 included examples of each.

Kurpfälzische, pre-1786
Leibfahne
White taffeta, with the Virgin holding the Christ-child and standing on the globe. Above her the motto SUB TUUM PRAESIDIUM VIRGO GLORIOSA. This central field is edged with a light blue and white flamed border; in each corner the yellow initials CT under an electoral cap and within

laurel branches (for 'Carl Theodor'). Below the Virgin is the Cross of the Order of the Lion of the Palatinate. A variation on this pattern had an edging with a triple row of light blue and white rhombi, with the corner motifs in the form of the Bavarian crest of lion, rhombi and orb.

Ordinär or Regimentsfahne
Red or yellow central field bearing the electoral crest with regalia on clouds, surrounded by trophies of arms and held by a lion passant. Beneath it the Cross of the Order of the Lion of the Palatinate, above it the motto DOMINUS VIRTUTUM VOBISCUM. Light blue and white rhombic edging. Another pattern is similar but with the lion, rhombi and orb as the central crest.

In 1786, after the unification of the electorates of Bavaria and the Palatinate, new flag designs were produced; the sizes were unchanged (1.73 metres square), and the designs were as follows:

Leibfahne, Obverse
As for the old pattern with triple light blue and white rhombic edging.

Leibfahne, Reverse
The great crest of Pfalz-Bayern with rampant lion supporters, beneath them the chains and crosses of the Orders of the Golden Fleece, St Hubert, the Lion of the Palatinate, and St George. The great crest was as follows (top to bottom, left to right):

Duchy of Cleve—golden wheel on red ground. Duchy of Jülich—black lion rampant on gold field. Duchy of Berg—red lion rampant on white ground. County of Mörs—horizontal black bar on gold field. Central position, Electorate of Bavaria—quartered gold lions rampant on black and light blue and white rhombi, central red shield bearing golden orb. County of Bergen-op-Zoom—three gold St Andrew's crosses on red field over three green hills. County of Mark—three horizontal rows of red and white dicing. Principality of Veldens—blue lion rampant on white field. County of Sponheim—three vertical rows of red and silver dicing. County of Ravensburg—three red chevrons on silver field. Edging as for Obverse.

Regimentsfahne
The great crest, as above, on a light blue ground, edging as for Leibfahne; both sides the same.

Lieutenant, 8th Infanterie-Regt. 'Herzog Pius', 1800–12. Weiland again fails to convey the height of the Raupenhelm, and shows an incorrect cuff: the Bavarian cuff had no flaps as such, it was simply split up the rear seam and held with four buttons. The imitation of embroidery on the gold lace collar bars is also misleading. Facings are sulphur yellow, buttons gold, sash and portepée silver and light blue. In early 1812 a gorget replaced the sash.

These new flags were to be painted. The first presentations took place in 1788. The scale of issue was reduced to one of each of the two types per regiment.

In 1799 the great crest on all new flags was altered to include the estates which fell to Pfalz-Bayern when, on the death of Elector Carl Theodor, the throne was assumed by Duke Maximilian Joseph of Pfalz-Zweibrücken, and the latter's troops were absorbed into the

Bavarian infantry bivouac, 1806–14; a contemporary plate from the 'Augsburger Bilder' series. The men at the left have cornflower blue coats faced with poppy red, and white buttons and buttonholes, which indicate the 1st (Leib) Regiment. The kneeling figure has red facings piped in white, and white buttons; the sleeping man is unidentifiable.

Bavarian army. The new additions to the great crest were the three crowned black ravens' heads on a silver field of the County of Rappolstein.

On 7 October 1801 the scale of flags was set at two Leib and two Ordinär; on 3 December 1803 this was changed to one Leib and three Ordinär; and on 31 March 1804, back to one of each type. As each regiment had two field battalions, the Leibfahne were carried by the first and the Ordinärfahne by the second battalions. This scale of flags was retained until 1918.

In 1803 it was decided to re-introduce embroidered flags, costlier but less fragile than the painted ones. Sometime between 1800 and 1803 the design of the Ordinärfahne was changed once again, in that instead of the great crest they showed on both sides the quartered Bavarian golden lions on black and light blue and white rhombi, with a red central shield bearing the golden orb; this was couched on palm and laurel branches and flanked by lions. This crest was on a light blue ground edged with the triple row of light blue and white rhombi—the actual number of rows on each flag varied, in practice, from two to four. In 1803 the Ordinärfahne was altered yet again to an overall pattern of light blue and white rhombi, the rows being sometimes vertical and sometimes horizontal. This pattern was re-issued in 1813.

Following the eclipse of the Holy Roman Empire, it was decided at the Reichsdeputationshauptschluss of 1803 that Catholic Bavaria would absorb several new territories, some of them Protestant. This led to a Cabinet Order of 3 December 1803 that the traditional Virgin and Child would vanish from the Leibfahne, to be replaced by the crest of the rulers of Bavaria—the Wittelsbachs. This was again the quartered lions and rhombi with the red central oval bearing the gold orb. The crest was on an ermine coat under an electoral cap, flanked by lions and couched on palm and laurel branches. The whole was on a white field surrounded by the triple rhombic edging. Surviving flags show many variations from this theoretical norm.

Flag staffs were brown, with light blue velvet covering. The cloth was nailed to the staff with gilt nails, and the gilt spearhead finials bore the following engravings or pierced patterns:

1777–99 CT (Elector Carl Theodor)
1799–1806 MJ (Elector Maximilian Joseph)
1806–1815 MJK (King Maximilian Joseph IV)

The staff ferrules were also gilt; and it seems that the flags were carried on plain white leather bandoliers. Blue and white silk cravats were presented with the flags, 1.06 metres long and 18cm wide; they were usually fringed with gold but were otherwise plain. It was common for commanders or colonels-in-chief to present cravats of their own, often richly embroidered with mottoes such as DER LIEBE UND FREUNDSCHAFT GEWIDMET ('Dedicated to love and friendship'); STREITET UND SIEGET FÜRS VATERLAND ('Fight and conquer for the Fatherland'); or the initials or family crests of the donors.

In 1806 the crest on the flags was altered yet again when Bavaria was elevated to the status of a kingdom by Napoleon, the electoral cap being replaced by a crown. On 2 July 1808 the central crest was simplified to show just light blue and white rhombi with, in the centre, a red shield bearing the gold orb over crossed sceptre and sword. The shield was flanked by lions rampant, each holding a flag staff with a light blue and white rhombic flag. The whole was on an ermine coat under a royal crown. This design was used in 1813 to replace those lost in Russia. They were carried on staffs covered in black leather.

Cavalry Standards
The Electoral Bavarian cavalry regiments carried standards dating from the time of Emperor Charles VII (1742–45), bearing on one side the double-headed eagle of the Holy Roman Empire, and on the other the quartered Wittelsbach crest. The regiments of the Palatinate retained their old standards after the 1786 unification. Four regiments of Chevau-Légers were raised by Graf Rumford in 1790, and three of these carried standards until 1803, when they were withdrawn. The fourth regiment existed only on paper. The scale of standards was one (white) Leibstandarte and three Eskadronsstandarten per regiment in 1790. In 1803 the dragoon guidons and Kürassier standards were reduced to one Leib and two Ordinär or Eskadronsstandarten (one per division of two squadrons). On 5 May 1803 this was reduced to one of each type per regiment; and on 31 March 1804 to one only per regiment, a Leibstandarte. In 1811 the two dragoon regiments then existing were converted to Chevau-Légers, handing in their remaining standards.

After the 1812–13 campaigns it was decided to raise three new heavy regiments, the Garde du Corps and 1st and 2nd Kürassiers, each with one Leib and two Divisionsstandarten. The Leibstandarten were white with gold embroidery and fringes; the others were light blue, that of the 2nd Division having silver embroidery and that of the 3rd having gold.

On the obverse of each standard was the crest as on the 1808 model Leibfahne, surrounded by laurel branches and with each corner filled with oak-leaves and acorns. On the reverse was the royal cypher MJK within a crowned laurel wreath. Garde du Corps standards did not have corner oak-leaves, but an edging of gold oak-leaves to all sides. The central medallions of the Kürassier Leibstandarten were silver, the edging and cypher of gold; these colours were reversed on their Ordinärstandarten.

The standards were from 40cm to 45cm square; the staffs were ribbed, and painted light blue; finials were as for infantry flags. Prior to 1815 bandoliers were of velvet of the regimental facing colour embroidered in the button colour. Each standard was decorated with gold cords and tassels, and plain light blue and white silk cravats with silver fringes. In 1815 both Kürassier bandoliers were light blue, while that of the Garde du Corps was black with gold embroidery—apparently an old item re-issued for economy. These standards may be seen in the Bavarian Army Museum at the castle of Ingolstadt.

The Plates

A: Trooper, Chevau-Légers-Regiment 'Fugger', 1792
Being light cavalry the saddle furniture of these regiments was cut in the Hungarian style—that is, with a long rear point to the schabraque and with a round portmanteau. Beneath the grey twill, buttoned overalls the man wears buff leather breeches and knee-boots. The sheepskin saddle cloth was edged in the coat colour for Chevau-Légers, in the facing colour for dragoons and Kürassiers. It should be noticed that the

Sketch of the calfskin pack; the only 'luggage' a soldier could take with him on campaign, it did not allow for many luxuries to be carried!

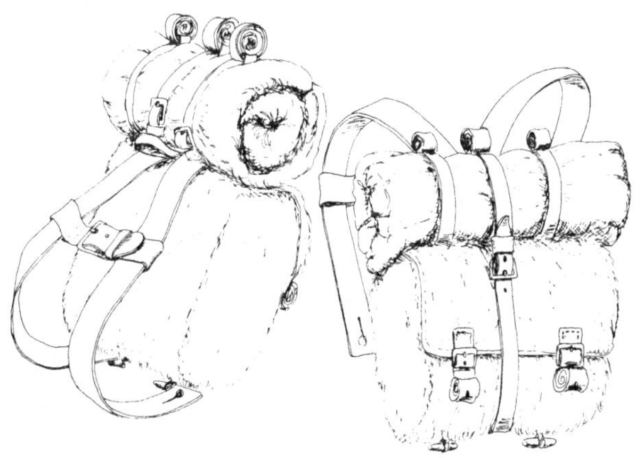

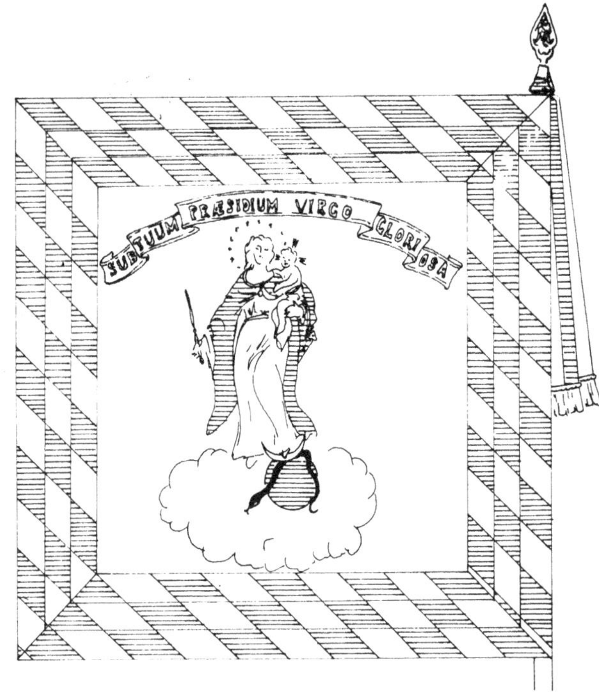

Bavarian infantry *Leibfahne*; the cloth is 1786 pattern, the tip 1806 pattern. A simple light blue and silver cravat is shown, but in practice these were elaborately embroidered.

Bavarian infantry *Ordinärfahne*, 1806 pattern, of light blue and white lozenges. This simple style replaced the elaborate crests previously carried in such chaotic profusion, and was retained until the end of the First World War; many examples survive in the Bavarian Army Museum at Ingolstadt.

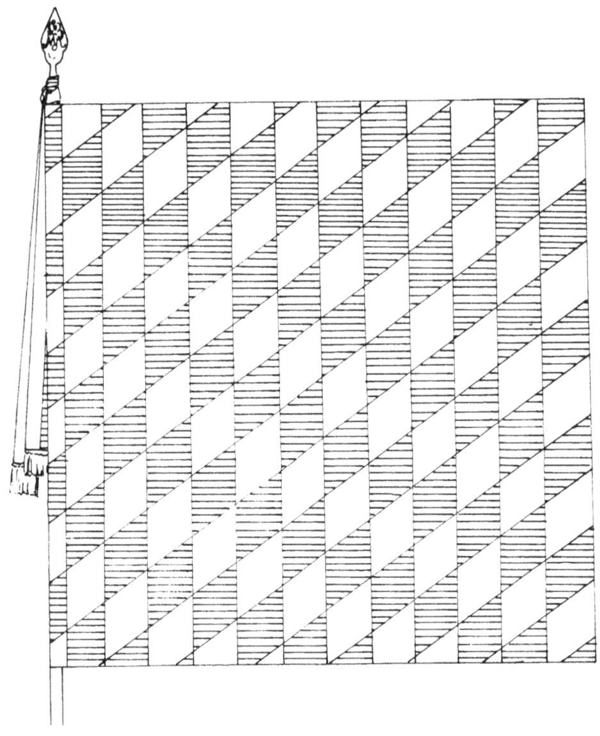

epaulettes were so designed that the button at the top end actually sat on the base of the collar rather than on the shoulder of the coat. Many contemporary plates show the epaulettes being worn far to the rear of the shoulder. (After Knötel, Volume XII, No. 9.)

B1: Captain, 5th Füsilier-Regiment 'von Wahl', 1792–99

This figure is based on a full-length portrait in the Bavarian Army Museum, Ingolstadt, where it is merely labelled 'Füsilier vom Regiment Wahl'—without any indication of rank. The details which lead us to the conclusion that this was a captain are the long turnbacks; the finer workmanship and the shorter peak on the helmet; the embroidered lapel buttonholes and the five lapel buttons; the light blue and silver sabre strap; the cane with gilt tip, and light blue and silver tassels and cord; and finally the boots instead of gaiters. Of particular interest are the fine black Hungarian thigh knots. The buff gloves are not on the original portrait but have been added. As well as designing uniforms and cannon, Graf Rumford also designed the sabre shown here; like the uniforms, the sabres were replaced in 1799.

B2: Colonel, 1st Feldjäger-Regiment 'von Schweicheldt', 1792–99

Rumford's experiences in the War of American Independence had proved to him the value of light troops as well as of practical uniforms. Not all members of these regiments were equipped with rifles, however; usually it was only one company per battalion. Rifles, although accurate, had the disadvantage that they quickly became fouled with the debris of gunpowder and cartridges, and this slowed their rate of fire considerably and quickly. The sombre colours of the uniforms were designed to aid concealment, although most soldiers of the day wore so many brightly polished appointments that these negated the benefits of the green and black uniform. The neighbouring state of Württemberg copied the Rumford uniforms very closely, as did the Prince of Condé in clothing his French émigré royalist corps, which was taken into Austrian service during this period. (After a portrait in the Bavarian Army Museum, Ingolstadt.)

B3: Drum-Major, 1st Füsilier-Regiment, 1790–99
While this haughty individual is uniformed in a superior manner, one of the main criticisms of Rumford's uniform was that it had the disadvantage for common infantrymen that if they waded a stream they could not take off their gaiters either before or afterwards (in order to stop them from getting wet or to dry them off if they were wet) because the gaiters were attached to the trousers. This meant that either the men went about naked from the waist down, or they preserved their dignity and risked sickness by wearing wet clothing. The cloth of which the coats were made was extremely thick—almost like felt—and the trouser-gaiters' material resembled sackcloth it was so coarse. The crest on the swallow's nests is the entwined 'MJ' on a crimson-lined ermine coat under the electoral cap.

C1: Captain, Horse Artillery, 1801–04
The artillery were the first to adopt the system of showing officers' ranks on the collar and it is noteworthy that this officer is wearing the Raupenhelm at a time when other officers were wearing the bicorn. The front plate of the helmet bears 'MJ' entwined under an electoral cap, and the cockade is in silver and light blue radial stripes—a pattern which was rapidly superseded by the concentric ring style. Another unusual feature of this figure is the black collar piped red; the artillery is usually shown with a red collar. The gilt shoulder-scales are of a type which was not seen in service for more than a year or two. Saddle furniture consisted of a red, Hungarian-style schabraque with gold edging and gold, crowned 'MJ' in front and rear corners. (After a contemporary painting in the Bavarian War Archives, München.)

C2: Füsilier Drummer, 2nd Line Infantry Regiment 'Kronprinz', 1807
It was common practice in all armies of this period to enlist young boys as drummers; they were often the sons of serving soldiers. They shared all the hardships of military life with their adult companions, and on campaign had to march with the rest or be abandoned. The 2nd Regiment wore black facings from 1799–1802 and carried the title 'Kurprinz' from 1799–1806. In 1814, when the Grenadier-Garde was raised, the 1st and 2nd Line Infantry Regiments lost the distinctive buttonhole lace decoration to lapels, cuffs and rear waist. On the red swallow's nests is the royal cypher 'MJK' on an ermine coat. The same crest is carried on the Raupenhelm plate and on the drum. Until 1799 the drums were of wood painted in light blue and white triangles. Cornflower blue was the traditional Bavarian infantry coat colour, which had been abandoned for the white of the Holy Roman Empire in 1785. From contemporary plates it would seem that some drummers wore tall, drooping red plumes and red fringed epaulettes. (After Müller and Braun.)

C3: Grenadier, 4th Line Infantry Regiment 'Salern', 1806
It is quite surprising that Bavarian élite com-

The cavalry bridle; students of horse-furniture will recognize the standard military pattern with halter and double reins.

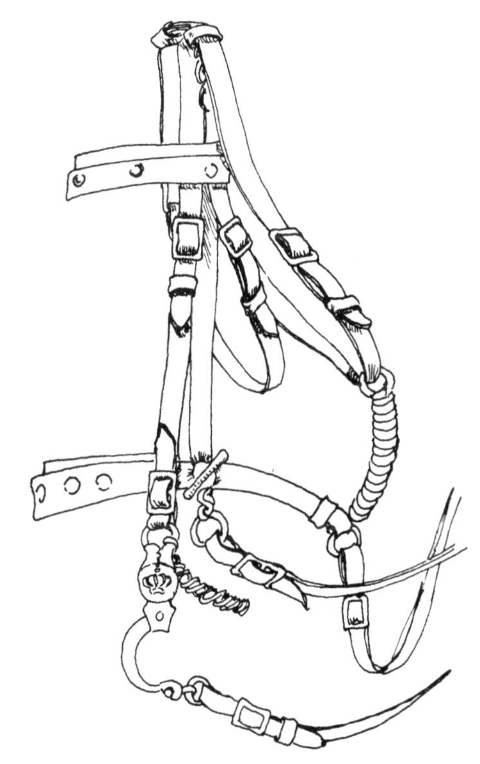

panies did not conform in uniform detail to their French equivalents (except in the matter of plume colour). The Bavarian grenadiers wore no fringed epaulettes and their sabres were without distinctive straps, but they were distinguished by a brass grenade on the pouch lid. Until 1807 the calfskin pack was carried on the left hip. In 1806 this regiment had red piping added to collar, lapels and cuffs which had previously been plain. The design of the cuff is as unique as that of the Raupenhelm. (After Müller and Braun.)

D: Trooper, 1st Dragoons, 1807

This plate is taken from one by Richard Knötel based on a picture in Schloss Schleissheim (Bavaria), which shows the regiment in action on 15 March 1807 before the Prussian fortress of Kosel in Silesia. The white parade breeches and high boots have been replaced for campaign wear by the grey buttoned overalls and short boots. The Raupenhelm is as for the infantry, but with the addition of the brass reinforcing bars over the top and back of the crown. The coat is as for the infantry, except that on the shoulders are white metal scales on a cloth backing in the facing colour, and the turnbacks are in the coat colour with only an edging in the facing colour. Saddle furniture is heavy cavalry pattern; the black and steel sabre sheaths were soon replaced with all-steel models. Contemporary plates show trumpeters of dragoons with red bearskin Raupenhelm crests. (After Müller and Braun.)

Bavarian infantry regimental colour—*Ordinärfahne*. The cloth of this flag is of the 1800 pattern, the gilt finial on the staff the 1806 pattern. Light blue and white borders enclose a white field bearing a red and white ermine cape showing the quartered arms of Bavaria (gold lion on black, blue/white lozenges) with a central golden orb on a red ground. The lions and the laurel and palm fronds are in natural colours.

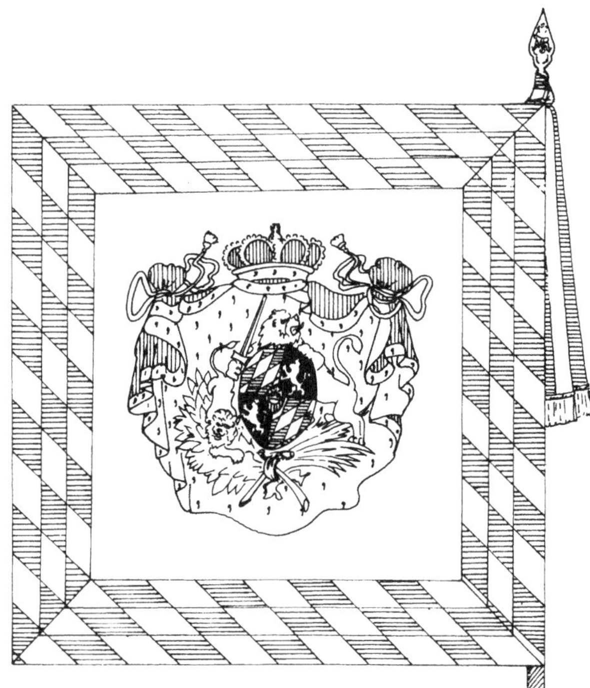

E1: 1st Lieutenant, 14th Line Infantry Regiment, 1809

In contrast to their counterparts in most other armies of this period, Bavarian infantry officers wore no epaulettes and retained the bulky, old-fashioned silver and light blue sash as a badge of office, together with the sabre strap in the same colours. Rank was shown by the large bearskin crest, the small lions' heads to either side of the Raupenhelm plate, and by the lace bars (in the button colour) on the collar. (After Müller and Braun.)

E2: Sergeant-Major, 2nd Chevau-Légers Regiment 'König', 1809

Senior NCO status is expressed here by the large, black bearskin crest, the absence of the carbine bandolier (which all junior NCOs and troopers wore), the cane, and the light blue and white striped sabre strap with a red wreath around the body of the tassel (obscured in this painting). The coat colour changed from light to dark green in 1809, and the style of the waistcoat was altered so that its peaks no longer showed under the bottoms of the lapels of the coat (as can be seen here). Senior NCOs and officers had helmets of superior quality to those of the men and with brass edging to the peak. On the red-edged turnbacks were white cloth crowns and rampant lions, as can be seen on plate F2. The cuffs were the usual Bavarian style, red with a vertical red piping. (After Müller and Braun.)

E3: Corporal, 3rd Füsilier Company, 11th Line Infantry Regiment 'Kinkel', 1810

Badges of office are not immediately obvious to outsiders, but consisted of the cane (carried hanging by its loop from the top lapel button), the

Bavarian Chevau-Légers swimming the River Niemen in 1812, a sketch made by Albrecht Adam at the time of the Grande Armée's invasion of Russia. The regiment is unidentifiable; but it is interesting to note the trumpeter on the grey in the right foreground, with a dropping helmet plume (red?) and 'wings' or false sleeves on the back of his jacket.

light blue and white sabre tassel and the three-bar sabre hilt. The company flash can be seen above the chinstrap boss. Since 1807 the calfskin pack had been carried over the shoulders on two straps, and seems to have been slightly enlarged from the previous size. Füsiliers wore no badges on the cartridge pouch. This was the uniform worn during the major campaigns of the Napoleonic Wars from 1805 to 1814; the Bavarians served in almost all theatres except for Spain. (After Müller and Braun.)

F1: Private, 4th Light Infantry Battalion 'Theobald', 1812

Apart from the coat and breeches colouring, Bavarian light infantry wore the same uniform as the line, and rank badges were of the same pattern. Instead of drummers the light infantry used buglers to pass commands, and the instruments were of the circular, continental model. When Karabinier companies were formed they wore a red plume on the left side of the helmet.

F2: 2nd Lieutenant, 1st Chevau-Légers-Regiment 'Kronprinz', 1809

This regiment was raised in 1803 from the cavalry of the Bishopric of Würzburg and remained in being even after Würzburg was handed over to Ferdinand of Austria in exchange for Salzburg in 1805. Until 1809 Chevau-Légers wore light green coats, thereafter dark green. Officers' appointments were as for those of dragoons, the main uniform peculiarity being in the white crowns and lions worn on the turnback corners. In 1812 all six Chevau-Légers regiments went with the main body of the Grande Armée to Moscow, and fought (and were destroyed) at Borodino. This had left the Bavarian corps with practically no cavalry when they were detached north to Polozk in July, and they suffered badly for the lack of it. (After Müller and Braun.)

F3: Captain, 1st Dragoons, 1806–11

This regiment became the 1st Chevau-Légers in 1811, and changed its uniform colour to dark green at that time. Troopers wore a wide red waist sash which fastened under the left arm with a pair of straps and buckles covered with a large red rosette. Badges of rank were as for the

Albrecht Adam made this sketch of Bavarian Chevau-Légers on the march in Russia in July 1812, a time of heat wave—note clouds of dust. The excellent formation shown here soon deteriorated as the horses weakened through lack of water, poor diet and forced marches. After Borodino these proud regiments were reduced to squadron strength.

infantry, with the exception that cavalry officers wore the silver and light blue striped bandolier with edging in the facing colour and with gilt picker equipment. The large white metal shoulder-scales gave protection against sabre cuts. (After Müller and Braun.)

G1: 2nd Lieutenant, Grenadier-Garde, 1815
Imitation is the sincerest form of flattery, and in 1815 the Bavarians raised not only three heavy cavalry regiments very much in the Imperial French style, but also this élite infantry unit which dressed in uniforms having a certain French flavour. The top patch of the bearskin bonnet was red with a white, upright cross, and the brass front plate bore the royal Bavarian arms with lion supporters, as did the silver gorget. On the red turnbacks were silver grenades (white for other ranks). Entry to this regiment was restricted to those who were of a certain minimum height and those who had distinguished war records. The white breeches and boots (or gaiters for other ranks) were worn for parades; in barracks they were replaced by cornflower blue trousers with a wide red side-stripe. (After Müller and Braun, and other contemporary sources.)

G2: 2nd Lieutenant, Uhlanen-Regiment, 1813
The costume (apart from the facing colour) is a straight copy of that worn by the Austrian Uhlans; and this regiment was raised in August 1813 when Bavaria had already decided to abandon Napoleon's cause and to join the allies (Prussia, Russia and Austria) whose armies were then gathering on Bavaria's eastern borders. In July 1814 the light blue facings were changed to

poppy red but the other details of the uniform were retained. An Austrian (a deserter from one of their Uhlan regiments) was engaged by the Bavarians to instruct the men in lance drill. The whole costume is an adaptation of the national costume of the native cavalry of Galicia (part of southern Poland in 1790)—a territory which was divided up between Prussia, Russia and Austria—and the Austrian Uhlans date from this annexation. The lance pennants were white over light blue. (After Müller and Braun.)

G3: Lieutenant-Colonel, 1st Kürassier-Regiment 'Prinz Karl', 1815

First issues of cuirasses to this regiment were made from stocks captured from the French, but the tall, heavy helmets were locally designed and produced. The elaborate gold oak-leaf decoration around the black sealskin turban was worn only by officers; other ranks had plain fur turbans and round chinstrap bosses in polished steel. Saddle furniture consisted for other ranks of red, square schabraque and portmanteau, both edged white, and a white sheepskin saddle cloth, edged red. Harness was black with brass fittings. Officers had silver edging to their red saddle furniture and their holster caps were covered in black bearskin. One senior officer of the 1st Kürassiers had suffered a head wound during the Russian campaign and could not bear the weight of the heavy helmet. He was given special permission to appear on duty in an old-fashioned bicorn. (After Müller and Braun, and other (contemporary) sources.)

H: Trumpeter, 1st Bavarian Hussars, 1815

The apple green shako, gold lace and buttons, red and gold sabretache and light blue schabraque are all hallmarks of the trumpeters of this regiment. The Landhusaren and Freiwillige-Husaren of 1813 and 1814 were temporary and voluntary formations, and were limited in the way in which they could be employed. The raising of the 1st and 2nd Hussars as part of the regular army provided permanent troops who could be used as and when necessary. It would seem that Austrian rather than French uniforms served as models for the dress of these regiments. Officers had silver edging to their saddle furniture and crowned silver cyphers 'MJK' in front and rear corners. Saddle and harness were Hungarian style. (After Müller and Braun, and other (contemporary) sources.)

A dying officer of Chevau-Légers at Borodino; Albrecht Adam has missed no detail of dress and equipment. The dying man's sash, pouch-belt, helmet and sabre lie beside him; and a trooper of the 10e Cuirassiers can be seen leading a wounded horse on the right.

INDEX

(References to illustrations are shown in **bold**. Plates are shown with caption locators in brackets.)

Printed and bound by CPI Group (UK) Ltd, Croydon, CR0 4YY

06/07/2026

02158996-0003